THE UNITED ★ STATES OF ★ PUZZLES

ERIC HARSHBARGER

PUZZLE
WRIGHT
PRESS

New York

PUZZLE WRIGHT PRESS

New York

An Imprint of Sterling Publishing Co., Inc.
1166 Avenue of the Americas
New York, NY 10036

ISBN 978-1-4549-3337-3

Distributed in Canada by Sterling Publishing Co., Inc.
c/o Canadian Manda Group, 664 Annette Street
Toronto, Ontario M6S 2C8, Canada
Distributed in the United Kingdom by GMC Distribution Services
Castle Place, 166 High Street, Lewes, East Sussex BN7 1XU, England
Distributed in Australia by NewSouth Books
University of New South Wales, Sydney, NSW 2052, Australia

For information about custom editions, special sales, and premium and corporate purchases,
please contact Sterling Special Sales at 800-805-5489 or specialsales@sterlingpublishing.com.

Manufactured in Canada

2   4   6   8   10   9   7   5   3   1

sterlingpublishing.com
puzzlewright.com

Cover design by David Ter-Avanesyan
Image credits are on page 124

★ ★ ★ CONTENTS ★ ★ ★

Introduction

There is a classic toy that most American children play with at some point growing up: a jigsaw puzzle with the pieces shaped as the United States. It is a wonderful toy that is both educational and entertaining.

In the early '80s, when trivia board games were a new fad, I remember a question in one of the games asking which of the 50 states has the longest name. The surprising answer is "Rhode Island and Providence Plantations" (the official name of that small state).

And who hasn't, at some point in their life, been quizzed about state capitals, whether on a geography test in school, or over a drink with friends at a pub.

Games and puzzles centered around the United States are not a new idea, but I hope that this book adds a plethora of entertaining challenges to the genre. For myself, the process of writing it has been the confluence of several personal interests.

First, there can be no doubt that I, Eric Harshbarger, am a puzzle nerd. I love puzzles. I enjoy solving puzzles, and I spend an inordinate amount of time creating puzzles. Paper and pencil puzzles, mysterious riddles, physical puzzles, scavenger hunts: I design them all, and have done so for many years.

For over a decade I organized annual "puzzle parties" in my hometown at which friends assembled into teams to spend a day solving conundrums and challenges specifically designed for them. Such events started as small affairs (about a dozen acquaintances solving puzzles for a few hours), but the final events were much larger in scope: overnight marathons, sometimes exceeding twenty-four hours, consisting of several dozen puzzles (obvious ones, hidden ones, "meta" ones, and so forth), with over a hundred people from around the country participating. They were very competitive parties, with exceptionally intelligent people all trying to accomplish some goal before the opposing teams beat them to it—with plenty of driving around town, looking for hidden objects, and, of course, solving more and more puzzles.

The parties were undoubtedly popular, and after years of organizing them, I realized that I had written quite a few puzzles that had referenced the United States. It dawned on me that a compilation of such challenges might be a worthwhile book to write.

But my affinity to such a project has even deeper roots. In addition to being a puzzle nerd, I could also be called, and I write this proudly, a true word nerd. I adore the English language; or more precisely, I adore its words. The grammar and semantics of it all I find interesting enough, but it's the vocabulary, the words themselves, that I truly love. The patterns of letters, the (often unusual) spellings, the phonetics, and the etymologies of words all fascinate me.

I was the geeky kid who could spend an entire afternoon doing nothing more than perusing an unabridged dictionary trying to spot unusual qualities about the entries on the printed page. Long before computer queries made such searching almost trivial, I would spend hours enraptured by large lexicons. I searched for all the words I could find that contained double I's ("skiing," "taxiing," "radii," "Hawaii," and so on). I looked for words that contained substrings of consecutive letters ("DEFine," "aFGHan," "undeR-STUdy"). Wordplay books such as Gyles Brandreth's *The Joy of Lex* and *More Joy of Lex* joined cherished dictionaries on my bookshelves. Other puzzle books by James F. Fixx (*Games for the Superintelligent*) and Christopher Manson (*Maze, The Practical Alchemist*) are, to this day, in my library next to works by Dmitri Borgmann, Ross Eckler, Martin Gardner, and the like.

This love of words is integral to my love of puzzles. And these interests eventually collided with another obsession of mine.

I love maps. Atlases, globes, and wall maps transfix me. I enjoy creating fictional maps. I am quite adept at spatial visualization. Reading maps and orienteering have always been very easy for me. I have a strong sense of direction; I rarely get lost. And, I appreciate the beauty and functionality of precisely drawn and skillfully labeled maps. The amount of useful information that can be packed into a well-designed map is often underappreciated.

The reader probably will not be surprised to learn that I have an eleven-by-eight foot road map of the United States hanging on a wall in my house, its laminated surface highlighted along all of the interstate highways I have driven upon. While I have not (yet) driven though all of the states, I have crisscrossed this vast country several times in an automobile. I first drove across America when I was just 17 years old. About ten years ago I managed to drive through 14 different states in just under 24 hours.

There are 50 states in this nation, and each has its own facts that are great fodder for puzzles: the names of the states, how they are spelled, how they can be sorted, how they are abbreviated—not to mention their histories full of trivia and their geographic positions in relation to one another. I tried my best to tap into all of this information when writing this book.

Not only should these pages provide hours of fun for solvers of all ages and skill levels, but I hope that teachers might appreciate the educational value of the book. I've tried to provide a great variety of puzzles. You will find all types herein: wordplay, number play, logic puzzles, a maze or two, and, of course, no shortage of maps. Some you will find to be simple, others might seem impossible; but, ideally, even the difficult ones you will find enjoyable—or at least intriguing. And if any require internet look-ups or deeper inquiry, I hope that research, too, is both enlightening and entertaining.

It was with great joy that I watched this book come together. In truth, I have always enjoyed creating puzzles more than solving them, so at no time during the authoring did I feel overwhelmed. It was gratifying to apply all of my nerdiness to such a focused endeavor and a wonderful experience from start to end.

But now my job is at that end. The puzzles have been written; the book has been published. And, thankfully, it is being read. Your job, the solving of the puzzles, is just beginning. I hope you derive as much pleasure from the book as I have already.

Good luck, and happy puzzling!

—Eric Harshbarger

About the Puzzles

Over the next hundred pages you will find the puzzles that constitute the main body of this book. There are many, many different types of puzzles included: some involve wordplay, others focus on mathematics and logic. There are visual puzzles and even a few games and challenges that do not have definitive answers. Many puzzles are variations of a single design; these have been scattered throughout the pages.

You will find a wide range of difficulties among all of the puzzles as well. Each page has a difficulty rating from one star ("easy") to five stars ("very difficult"). There is a Hints section near the end of the book (before a few helpful Appendices) that provides clues to some of the puzzles without giving away the final answers. Not all of the puzzles have hints, but for the ones that do, the 1-to-5 star rating will display some of its stars as an outline. Those stars give a rough indication of how helpful the hint is. For example, if a puzzle's difficulty rating is "★★★☆" then you can estimate that without the hint the puzzle has a 4-star difficulty, but that if you read the associated hint, then the challenge will decrease to about 3 stars. If a puzzle's difficulty rating consists of all solid red stars, then no hint is available. Some puzzles have a "mixed bag" rating of "★★" indicating that it is a multi-part challenge of varying difficulty (for example, a list of trivia questions). Of course, these ratings are very subjective, and you may find that you have a stronger affinity toward one class of puzzles than to another.

Finally, starting on page 108 you will find the answers to all of the puzzles. Some of those answers include additional information about a puzzle, its history, or construction. (All facts are accurate as of May 2019, but some will change over time, of course.)

Acknowledgments

Thanks to the many friends and family members who, through the years, have enthusiastically play-tested and solved so many of my puzzles. Special thanks to Tracy Cobbs and Wil Zambole, who originally puzzled me with some of the state-related trivia questions I included in this book, and to Francis Heaney at Puzzlewright Press for helpful edits and tweaks.

State Packing

Can you fit the names of all 50 states into the grid below? Ignore any spaces within state names (e.g. consider "NEW YORK" as just "NEWYORK"). If needed, a list of all 50 states is provided in Appendix A at the back of this book.

Perfectly Stated Puzzles

The small words IN, ME, and OR are all simple examples of words that can be spelled by using only the two-letter abbreviations of states (Indiana, Maine, and Oregon, respectively). Other, longer words (with even lengths, of course) may also be found; for example, CAME (California + Maine), HIDE (Hawaii + Delaware), and ORDEAL (Oregon + Delaware + Alabama). Below are clues to several more such words; can you figure out what the answers are?

Two-state answers:
- Fluids for pens ___ ___
- Volcanic discharge ___ ___
- Not humid ___ ___
- Wizard's device ___ ___
- Stocking stuffer for naughty children ___ ___
- Units of resistance ___ ___
- Penny, dime, or quarter, e.g. ___ ___
- (Mostly) daily delivery ___ ___

Three-state answers:
- Enter territory in a hostile manner ___ ___ ___
- Sounds that warn of danger ___ ___ ___
- One who damages or destroys works of art ___ ___ ___
- Sweet liquid of flowers ___ ___ ___
- Computer networking devices ___ ___ ___
- Solve, as a cipher ___ ___ ___

Four-state answers:
- Culinary dish made of squid ___ ___ ___ ___
- Relating to a certain mosquito-borne disease ___ ___ ___ ___

All Over the Map

Can you determine the reasoning used to enumerate the states in the map below? The rationale may be geographical, logological, historical, or anything else. If you're stuck, check the Hints section for a clue.

Pentomino Puzzle: Kentucky ★★★

Pentominoes are geometric shapes formed by adjoining five squares edge to edge. There are twelve different pentomino shapes (shown at right), which may be rotated or flipped over or both. Can you arrange the twelve pentominoes to make the shape of Kentucky? Multiple solutions are possible. (If you do not have physical pentomino pieces, see Appendix C.)

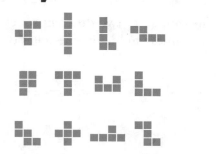

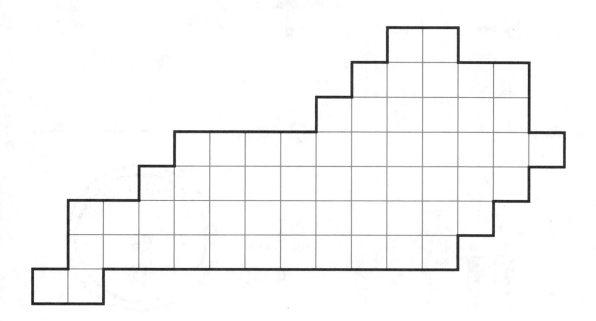

Capital Cartoons

The capitals of two different states are depicted below in rebus form. Can you guess the city names (and name the states of which they are the capitals)?

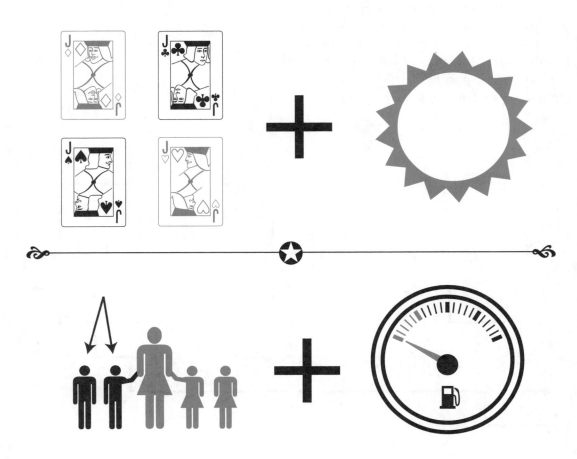

County Lines: Arizona

The names of all 15 counties of Arizona are hidden in the grid below (vertically, horizontally, diagonally, and reversed), ignoring spaces. After you find them all, the leftover letters will spell two facts about Arizona.

```
        A  R  L  I  Z  O  N  G  A  E  S
        S  T  A  A  T  E  A  F  I  E  L
  O     W  E  N  R  I  P  S  T  H  L  E
  S  A  O  N  I  N  O  C  O  C  G  N  A
     U  A  R  P  C  O  C  A  C  T  E  U
     S  B  L  I  O  O  S  S  O  V  E  M
        I  R  A  T  A  C  L  A  S  R  O
        A  H  P  L  A  S  H  I  M  G  T
     M  S  V  A  E  R  O  G  I  Y  I  O
     W  N  P  V  O  M  F  R  F  S  I  P
  C  I  A  A  A  L  A  P  A  C  H  E  S
  T  Z  A  T  Y  E  N  E  H  C  K  W  E
  A  R  T  Z  U  R  C  A  T  N  A  S
        H  E  B  M  O  M  L  A  T  I
           N  A  V  A  J  O  E
```

APACHE
COCHISE
COCONINO
GILA
GRAHAM
GREENLEE
LA PAZ
MARICOPA
MOHAVE
NAVAJO
PIMA
PINAL
SANTA CRUZ
YAVAPAI
YUMA

Feeling Dotty ★★

Connect the dots below, in order, and you will draw a flag of one of the U.S. states. Can you identify which state's it is? If not, you may decode the answer by anagramming the letters that have not been crossed out once the dots are connected.

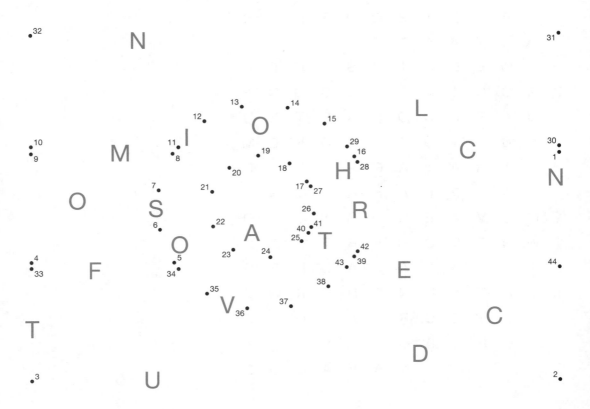

All Over the Map 2

Can you determine the reasoning used to enumerate the states in the map below? The rationale may be geographical, logological, historical, or anything else. If you're stuck, check the Hints section for a clue.

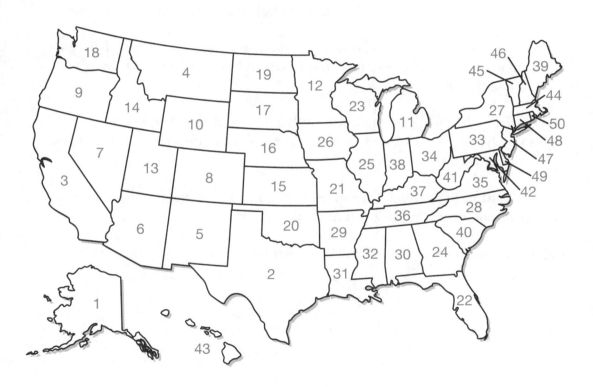

State the Facts

Three men (Frank, Harris, and Paul) and two women (Helen and June) are chatting at the office one day and realize that they all spent their childhoods in different states. After a bit more discussion the following facts come to light:

1. Their surnames are Columbus, Denver, Jackson, Lincoln, and Montgomery.

2. Mr. Denver grew up in a house overlooking the Mississippi River, Helen grew up on the shore of one of the Great Lakes, and June did not grow up in a landlocked state.

3. After high school Paul finally left his home state, though barely, since he simply went to an adjacent one (the home of one of the other men) to attend college at Auburn University.

4. The name of the capital of each person's home state either matches their last name or it contains their first name as a substring.

Can you determine each person's full name and home state?

A Commonplace Puzzle

Below, three state outlines have been overlaid atop one another (they are not drawn with a consistent scale). The dot represents a city, town, or village at that location within each particular state. The place's name is the same for all of the states. Can you identify the locale? Here's more help: The second letters of each state's name may be anagrammed into the name of the highlighted location.

State Assembly

When the six jigsaw puzzles pieces shown below are assembled, the red figure will form a silhouette of one of the 50 states (with its capital indicated by a star). Can you determine which state it is? If you have a hard time mentally moving the pieces about, you may try using some tracing paper to reconstruct the pieces into an assembled solution.

Pentomino Puzzle: Massachusetts ★★★

Pentominoes are geometric shapes formed by adjoining five squares edge to edge. There are twelve different pentomino shapes (shown at right), which may be rotated or flipped over or both. Can you arrange the twelve pentominoes to make the shape of Massachusetts? Multiple solutions are possible. (If you do not have physical pentomino pieces, see Appendix C.)

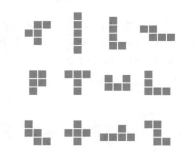

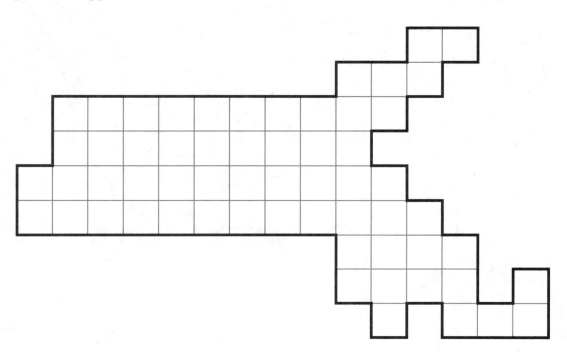

All Over the Map 3

Can you determine the reasoning used to enumerate the states in the map below? The rationale may be geographical, logological, historical, or anything else. If you're stuck, check the Hints section for a clue.

Popularity Contest: California

California is home to more people than any other state in the United States. Below is a blanked-out list of the 10 most populous cities of the Golden State, sorted by population with the largest at the top. Can you fill in the proper city names? If two or more vertically aligned cells share the same letter, they have been merged.

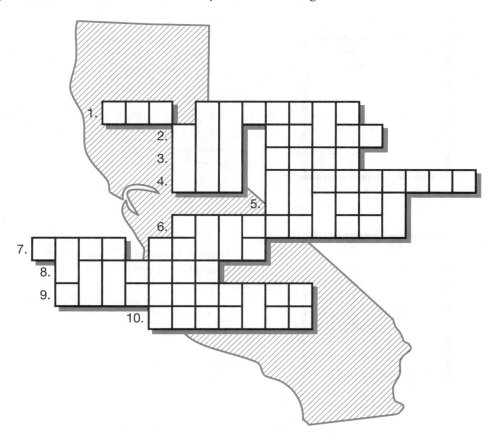

Squared Away

Clues are provided to help you complete the small crossword puzzles below. However, each answer is a five-letter word, and some of the cells must have two letters written in them. Any such bigrams entered will be two-letter postal abbreviations of U.S. states.

ACROSS
1 Joe that isn't joltin'?
4 Shady garden retreat
5 Descends into water

DOWN
1 Sweethearts
2 Dwelling in the woods
3 Spoons' companions

ACROSS
1 Hammett creation
4 Lessens in intensity
5 They may be made with cashews

DOWN
1 A Hindu holy man
2 Committee
3 Classroom furniture

Trivial Statements

Here are a few of my favorite trivia questions concerning U.S. states and wordplay. See how many of them you can answer.

1. Which states are spelled using only letters from the first half of the alphabet?

2. How many state names end with the letter K?

3. Which is the only state name that can be typed using just the left hand when adhering to "proper typing form" and using a standard QWERTY keyboard? How about when using only the right hand? Which is the only state name that can be typed using just keys from a single row of a keyboard?

4. Which state name shares no letters with its capital's name?

5. Sixteen states have two-letter postal abbreviations that match chemical symbols from the periodic table of elements. How many of these states (and elements) can you name?

6. No state name may be perfectly spelled by concatenating two-letter postal abbreviations (see page 9 for a puzzle concerning words that do have this property). However, there are a few states that may be so spelled if you allow extra letters to remain at the beginning and/or end of the construction. One example is FL-OR-ID-AR. What are the others?

Chemically Altered States

You've likely never noticed this before, but the phrase "United States of America" may be written using various symbols from the periodic table of elements. There are two slightly different ways it can be done, actually, and here they are:

92	28	52	110	73	52	16
U	Ni	Te	Ds	Ta	Te	S
Uranium	Nickel	Tellurium	Darmstadtium	Tantalum	Tellurium	Sulfur

92	7	53	52	110	73	52	16
U	N	I	Te	Ds	Ta	Te	S
Uranium	Nitrogen	Iodine	Tellurium	Darmstadtium	Tantalum	Tellurium	Sulfur

I'm happy to report that my name can also be represented (though this has only been possible since 2004 when Roentgenium officially got its symbol):

68	53	6
Er	I	C
Erbium	Iodine	Carbon

So, the obvious question now is, how many of the 50 state names may be constructed using chemical element symbols? If you do not have a periodic table just lying around for reference, a list of elements and their abbreviations has been provided for you in Appendix B of this book. You will find that for all but one of the possible constructions the answer is unique; one state, however, can be spelled using nine different arrangement of chemical symbols—see if you can figure out all of them!

8	9	95	68	53	20
O	F	Am	Er	I	Ca
Oxygen	Fluorine	Americium	Erbium	Iodine	Calcium

8	9	95	68	53	20
O	F	Am	Er	I	Ca
Oxygen	Fluorine	Americium	Erbium	Iodine	Calcium

1	18	16	1	56	111	68
H	Ar	S	H	Ba	Rg	Er
Hydrogen	Argon	Sulfur	Hydrogen	Barium	Roentgenium	Erbium

All Over the Map 4

Can you determine the reasoning used to enumerate the states in the map below? The rationale may be geographical, logological, historical, or anything else. If you're stuck, check the Hints section for a clue.

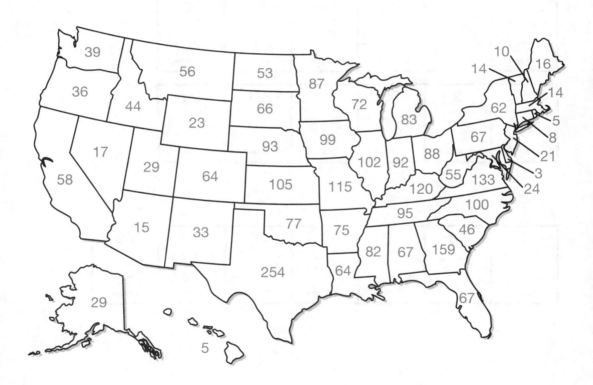

Perplex-cities: Colors

America is such a vast country, and its states so diverse, that we are blessed with wonderfully eclectic names when it comes to cities, towns, and other locations. Monikers in the northeast reflect the English, Dutch, German, and other heritages of the first settlers of that region, while the southwest exhibits a strong Spanish influence. And, of course, throughout the nation, place names were often derived from the many Native American peoples who inhabited the land.

Inspired by this great variety, I anagrammed the names of 11 U.S. place names that each contain a color, changing them into place names that are colorful in a different sense. Can you figure out the genuine names of the following locales? (The enumerations of the answers are given in the hint section, along with some solving strategies.)

1. **Blown Livers**, Texas (a city of 175,023 people, according to the 2010 census)
2. **Boggle Winner**, Kentucky (a city of 58,067)
3. **Ten-Sail Whip**, New York (a city of 56,853)
4. **Sundae Bill**, Illinois (a city of 23,706)
5. **Urban Gorge**, South Carolina (a city of 13,964)
6. **Castle Knob**, Massachusetts (a town of 9,026)
7. **Fool Dawdlers**, Minnesota (a city of 5,254)
8. **Pressingly Low**, Ohio (a village of 3,487)
9. **Silly Grave**, Alabama (a city of 2,165)
10. **Phil Kiln**, North Carolina (a town of 552)
11. **Glue Papers**, Wyoming (a "census designated place" of 535 people)

Sum of Its Parts

In the addition problem below, the digits have been replaced by letters (each letter represents the same number throughout the problem). Using mathematics, logic, and a bit of trial and error, can you determine the unique equation?

$$
\begin{array}{r}
\text{F I F T Y} \\
+ \text{S T A T E S} \\
\hline
\text{A M E R I C A}
\end{array}
$$

0 1 2 3 4 5 6 7 8 9

Pentomino Puzzle: Utah

Pentominoes are geometric shapes formed by adjoining five squares edge to edge. There are twelve different pentomino shapes (shown below), which may be rotated or flipped over or both. Can you arrange the twelve pentominoes to make the shape of Utah? Multiple solutions are possible. (If you do not have physical pentomino pieces, see Appendix C.)

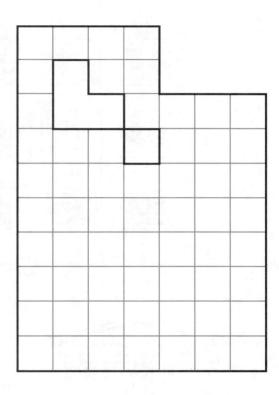

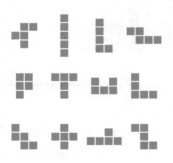

Capital Cartoons 2

The capitals of two different states are depicted below in rebus form. Can you guess the city names (and name the states of which they are the capitals)?

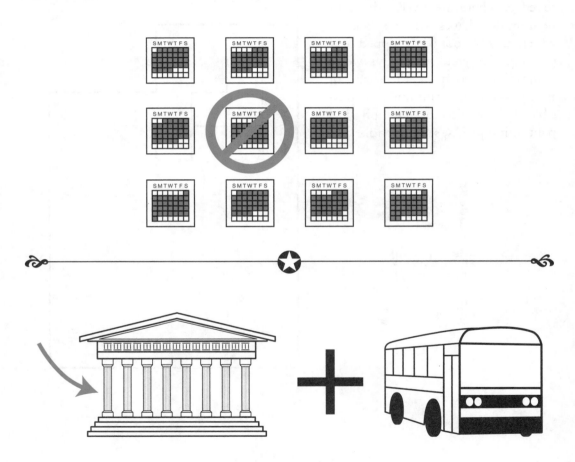

All Over the Map 5

Can you determine the reasoning used to enumerate the states in the map below? The rationale may be geographical, logological, historical, or anything else. If you're stuck, check the Hints section for a clue.

A Commonplace Puzzle 2

Below, five state outlines have been overlaid atop one another (they are not drawn with a consistent scale). The dot represents a city, town, or village at that location within each particular state. The place's name is the same for all of the states. Can you identify the locale? Here's more help: The second letters of each state's name may be anagrammed into the name of the highlighted location.

State Assembly 2

When the eight jigsaw puzzles pieces shown below are assembled, the red figure will form a silhouette of one of the 50 states (with its capital indicated by a star). Can you determine which state it is? If you have a hard time mentally moving the pieces about, you may try using some tracing paper to reconstruct the pieces into an assembled solution.

That's My Motto

The letters at the top of each column have been removed from the spaces below and sorted alphabetically. If you drop the letters back into their proper squares, then a message can be read in the grid from left to right, top to bottom, with words separated by blue squares (words can wrap around the right edge of the grid). The resulting message is the official motto of one of the U.S. states. Furthermore, the letters appearing in the squares highlighted with red will spell the name of the state that uses this particular motto.

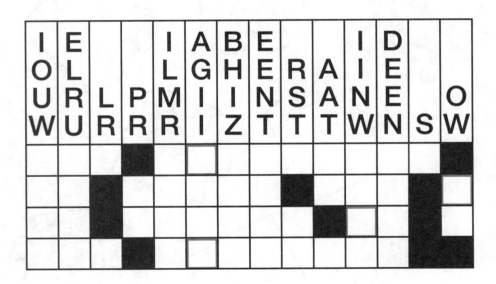

County Lines: New Jersey

The names of all 21 counties of New Jersey are hidden in the grid below (vertically, horizontally, diagonally, and reversed), ignoring spaces. After you find them all, the leftover letters will spell a fact about New Jersey.

```
            H N
          E W U J E
        R S C A M D E N E
      Y N O I N U E S S E X
        A H T U O M N O M D
      A E K N A S T H Y N E
      G C I A S S A P A A
        O R L D O E L M
        N S T T M R A E T
        E A H E A S P M M
          O B R R M A E U R
          M U S B I C A N R
        A U R R E E D A B E
      Y C P E L T R D C T E
    N M O R R I S T L S A
  N O D R E T N U H E G E
T H N A E N A G L C S X
L O T E C H E T U R E S
  N E G R E B O T S X
    A T E R L N S
      M G A U
          S W
        E S
```

ATLANTIC
BERGEN
BURLINGTON
CAMDEN
CAPE MAY
CUMBERLAND
ESSEX
GLOUCESTER
HUDSON
HUNTERDON
MERCER
MIDDLESEX
MONMOUTH
MORRIS
OCEAN
PASSAIC
SALEM
SOMERSET
SUSSEX
UNION
WARREN

All Over the Map 6

Can you determine the reasoning used to enumerate the states in the map below? The rationale may be geographical, logological, historical, or anything else. If you're stuck, check the Hints section for a clue.

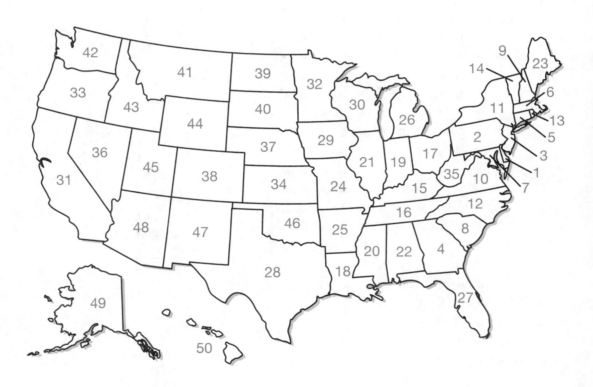

Pentomino Puzzle: Nebraska ★★★

Pentominoes are geometric shapes formed by adjoining five squares edge to edge. There are twelve different pentomino shapes (shown at right), which may be rotated or flipped over or both. Can you arrange the twelve pentominoes to make the shape of Nebraska? Multiple solutions are possible. (If you do not have physical pentomino pieces, see Appendix C.)

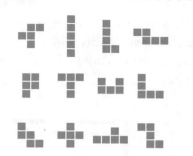

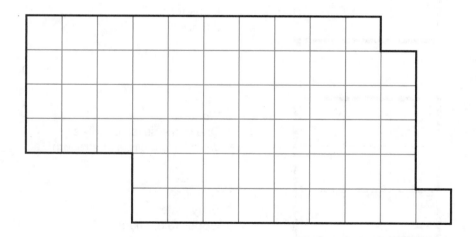

Squared Away 2

Clues are provided to help you complete the small crossword puzzles below. However, each answer is a five- or six-letter word, and some of the cells must have two letters written in them. Any such bigrams entered will be two-letter postal abbreviations of U.S. states.

ACROSS
1 Ten-year period
4 "World," to the French
5 Standards or averages

DOWN
1 Evil spirit
2 Frankness
3 Judges

ACROSS
1 Work
4 One of the seven deadly sins
5 Word before circle or strength

DOWN
1 Rabbit
2 Salty water
3 Opposite of chaos

Vexing Vexillology

"Vexillology" is an unusual looking word that simply means "the study of flags." This vexing puzzle presents you with several strange flags and asks you to identify the authentic design. Below are twelve flags, but only one of them correctly represents the current flag of the United States. Which flag is the true one?

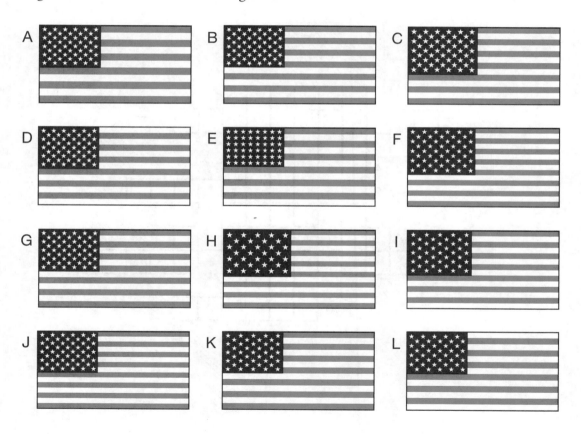

Popularity Contest: Texas

Texas is the second most populous state in the United States. Below is a blanked-out list of the 10 most populous cities of the Lone Star State, sorted by population with the largest at the top. Can you fill in the proper city names? If two or more vertically aligned cells share the same letter, they have been merged.

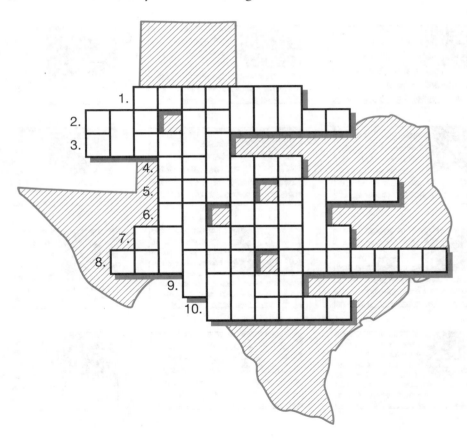

All Over the Map 7

Can you determine the reasoning used to enumerate the states in the map below? The rationale may be geographical, logological, historical, or anything else. If you're stuck, check the Hints section for a clue.

41

Map Coloring

If you have four crayons or colored pencils handy,* here's a challenge to keep you busy: color this map of states in such a way that each state is a single color, but no two adjacent states are the same color. You're going to need all four colors to do this, but if you're careful, you should not need a fifth.

* If you don't, you can simply label the states with the numbers 1, 2, 3, and 4 instead.

A couple more notes about borders: first, use only one color for each state even if that state has separated areas (like the islands of Hawaii, or the two sections of Michigan). Second, it's up to you whether you want the touching-only-at-corners states at the Four Corners region to be considered "bordering" or not; the challenge is solvable either way. However, it is more difficult if you adopt the rule that the diagonally adjacent states in that location (such as Utah and New Mexico) must be different colors.

Capital Cartoons 3

The capitals of two different states are depicted below in rebus form. Can you guess the city names (and name the states of which they are the capitals)?

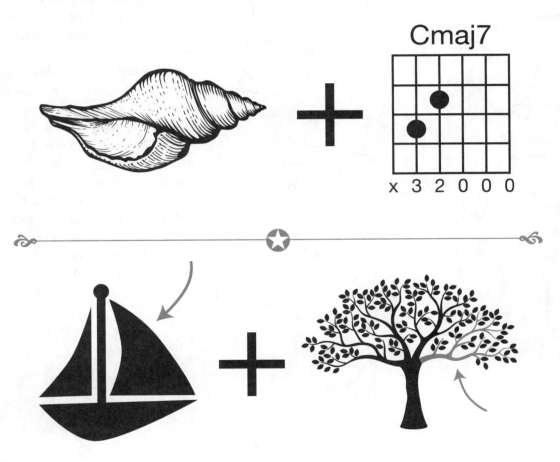

Feeling Dotty 2

Connect the dots below, in order, and you will draw a flag of one of the U.S. states. Can you identify which state's it is? If not, you may decode the answer by anagramming the letters that have not been crossed out once the dots are connected.

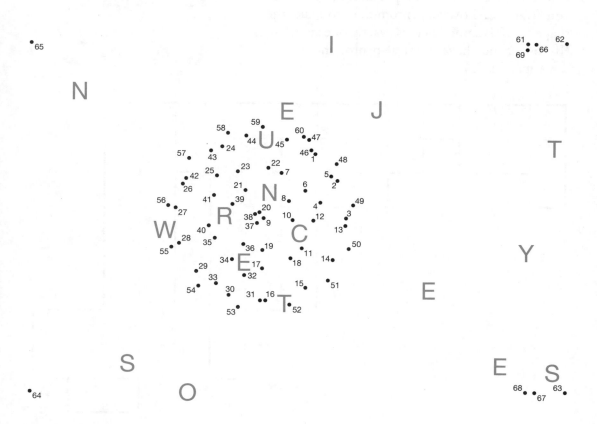

Pentomino Puzzle: Maryland ★★★

Pentominoes are geometric shapes formed by adjoining five squares edge to edge. There are twelve different pentomino shapes (shown at right), which may be rotated or flipped over or both. Can you arrange the twelve pentominoes to make the shape of Maryland? There is exactly one solution. (If you do not have physical pentomino pieces, see Appendix C.)

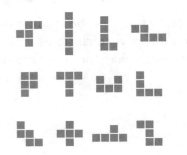

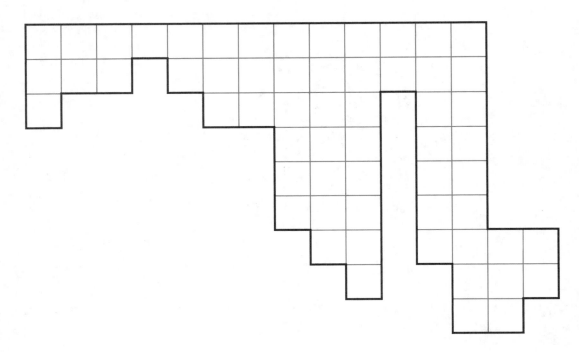

State the Facts 2

Five husbands (Charles, Jeff, Marc, Pierre, and Trent) and their wives (Cheyenne, Diana, Helen, Lulu, and Madison) spent the afternoon together at a Fourth of July cookout. By the time they watched the fireworks that evening they had learned the following facts:

1. Each couple was married in a state whose capital's name contained either the name of the bride or the groom.

2. At least two states beginning with the letter W hosted a wedding.

3. Marc's wedding was in a state that bordered the one in which Cheyenne got married.

4. Trent's wedding ceremony was at a location westernmost of all in question, while Helen's was the easternmost.

5. Madison is married to neither Charles nor Marc.

Can you determine who is married to whom and in which states their weddings were held?

All Over the Map 8

★★☆☆

Can you determine the reasoning used to enumerate the states in the map below? The rationale may be geographical, logological, historical, or anything else. If you're stuck, check the Hints section for a clue.

Trivial Statements 2

Here are a few more trivia questions, this time focusing on names of certain cities within the United States. Try to answer them and then quiz your friends.

1. Which four state capital names end with the word "City"?

2. What is the most populous U.S. city whose name is only one syllable long?

3. What is the most populous U.S. city that is not directly served by the Interstate Highway System?

4. Honolulu, Hawaii, is the southernmost state capital in the United States. But if only the contiguous forty-eight states are considered, which state capital is farthest south?

5. What is the most populous U.S. city with a Q in its name?

6. Logologically, what is unique about the city of Mockingbird Valley (located in the state of Kentucky)?

7. In which state will you find the town of Kansas located within the county of Delaware? In what other state will you find the town of Wyoming in the county of Iowa?

8. What is the only U.S. city, town, or village name that begins with an X?

A Hardscrabble Challenge

There's a good chance you have a copy of the ever-popular Scrabble game in your home; if you do, you might want to find the box and grab the bag of 100 tiles for this puzzle. If not, I've listed all of the letter tiles below. Your challenge is to use those 100 tiles to create a list of as many U.S. state names as possible. Just a list, though: no crossing words and no sharing tiles between words. Simply spell out as many of the states as you can, without repeating any of the names in your list. The two blank tiles may be designated as whatever letters you wish, and any spaces in state names should be ignored.

Your goal is to try to create as long a list of states as possible. The answer in the back of the book will show my list of twelve state names. Can you match (or better) that?

All Over the Map 9

Can you determine the reasoning used to enumerate the states in the map below? The rationale may be geographical, logological, historical, or anything else. If you're stuck, check the Hints section for a clue.

State Songs

Popular songs of all eras and genres have often included the names of U.S. states within their titles. "Tennessee" and "Texas" seem to be the most popular when it comes to country music, while "California" is most often named in pop and rock songs.

But many other states have also gotten their moments in the limelight. How many of the following song titles can you identify? Each contains the indicated state names.

If you need more clues about the songs' titles, check the Hints section.

In 1985 Marie Osmond sang this #1 country hit with Dan Seals.

Jamie O'Neal just reached the Top 40 pop chart with this song in early 2001.

In 1947 Frank Sinatra sang a popular song whose title includes both of these states.

This classic rock song by the Eagles topped the charts in 1977.

Mitch Miller & His Orchestra had a huge #1 hit about this big state back in 1955.

This 1969 instrumental hit by the Ventures was the theme of a popular television show and reached #4 on the charts.

Loretta Lynn and Conway Twitty sang a #1 country duet in 1973 whose title mentions two states.

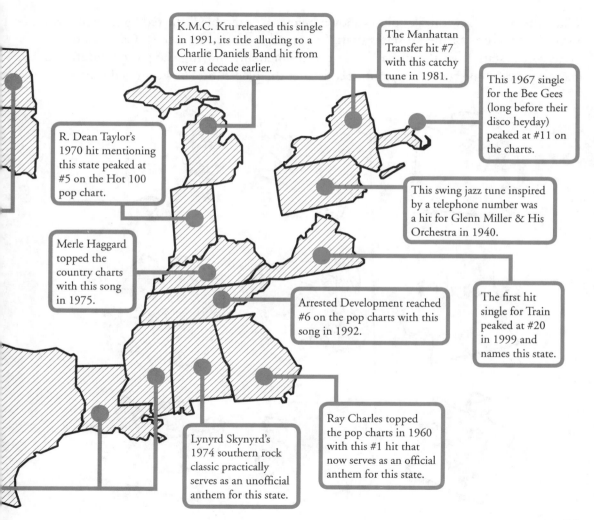

K.M.C. Kru released this single in 1991, its title alluding to a Charlie Daniels Band hit from over a decade earlier.

The Manhattan Transfer hit #7 with this catchy tune in 1981.

This 1967 single for the Bee Gees (long before their disco heyday) peaked at #11 on the charts.

R. Dean Taylor's 1970 hit mentioning this state peaked at #5 on the Hot 100 pop chart.

This swing jazz tune inspired by a telephone number was a hit for Glenn Miller & His Orchestra in 1940.

Merle Haggard topped the country charts with this song in 1975.

Arrested Development reached #6 on the pop charts with this song in 1992.

The first hit single for Train peaked at #20 in 1999 and names this state.

Lynyrd Skynyrd's 1974 southern rock classic practically serves as an unofficial anthem for this state.

Ray Charles topped the pop charts in 1960 with this #1 hit that now serves as an official anthem for this state.

State Assembly 3

When the nine jigsaw puzzles pieces shown below are assembled, the red figure will form a silhouette of one of the 50 states (with its capital indicated by a star). Can you determine which state it is? If you have a hard time mentally moving the pieces about, you may try using some tracing paper to reconstruct the pieces into an assembled solution.

54

United States of Algebra

The numbers 1 through 26 have been assigned, in some order, to the letters A through Z. The name of each state has then had the values of all its letters added together, with the resulting sum placed in the map below. Can you determine what value must have been assigned to the letter Q?

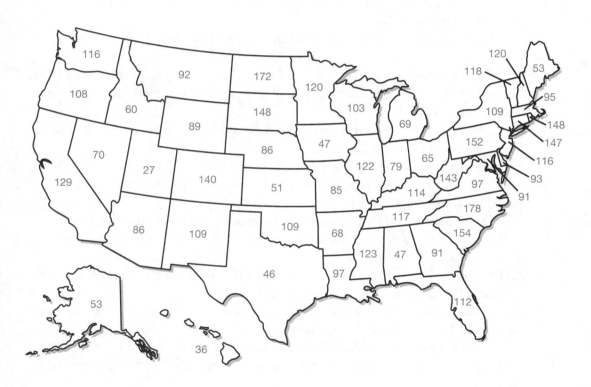

Additional Trivial Statements

For each of the following trivia clues, take one of the state names listed in the box on the far right, add the indicated letters, and anagram to find the answer. For instance, given the instruction "Add **BC** to a state to get a famous fictional Crane," you would anagram BC + IDAHO to get ICHABOD. Can you solve them all?

1. Add **AL** to a state to get the children's author who also wrote the 1921 Broadway play "Mr. Pim Passes By."
2. Add **DR** to a state to get the author of the poem "The Dong With a Luminous Nose."
3. Add **FL** to a state to get the second cereal created by Kellogg's, introduced in 1915.
4. Add **GM** to a state to get the cute type of creature that can turn into a gremlin, in the movie "Gremlins."
5. Add **GO** to a state to get an actor who has played Count Dracula, Ludwig van Beethoven, and Winston Churchill.
6. Add **HI** to a state to get the capital of the Democratic Republic of the Congo.
7. Add **HT** to a state to get the last name of Olympic skier Gus, who won a silver medal for slopestyle in 2014.
8. Add **IM** to a state to get an Apache warrior whose name became a battle cry.
9. Add **IR** to a state to get the title character of a series of French comics set in ancient Gaul.
10. Add **IY** (and an accent mark) to a state to get the third book of the trilogy that includes "O Pioneers!" and "The Song of the Lark."
11. Add **JN** to a state to get the name of a pageant, as it was familiarly known, that is now called Distinguished Young Women.
12. Add **JY** to a state to get a Hank Williams song subtitled "On the Bayou."
13. Add **NS** to a state to get part of a marine animal associated with the theme from "Jaws."

14. Add **NT** to a state to get the name of the leader who succeeded Dag Hammarskjöld.
15. Add **PW** to a state to get the first name by which Caryn Elaine Johnson is better known.
16. Add **ST** to a state to get the character played by Sophie Turner on "Game of Thrones."
17. Add **ACR** to a state to get the company whose mascot is Dino the brontosaurus.
18. Add **AES** to a state to get the fictional business once re-themed as the British pub "The Nag and Weasel."
19. Add **AGY** to a state to get a Bing Crosby movie in which he sang "Swinging on a Star."
20. Add **ALM** to a state to get the singer who played Enrico Caruso in 1951's "The Great Caruso."
21. Add **AVY** to a state to get a company that's sold products including the Hummer, Topper, Bobcat, and Breakout.
22. Add **ETV** to a state to get the more common name of the flower sometimes called "saintpaulia."
23. Add **HSU** to a state to get the actor who played the son of Kelly McGillis's character in the movie "Witness."
24. Add **LSW** to a state to get the city that's the headquarters of R.J. Reynolds.
25. Add **VVY** to a state to get iridium's atomic number.
26. Add **EENT** to a state to get the poem that includes the line "I shall be telling this with a sigh / Somewhere ages and ages hence."

ALABAMA
ALASKA
ARKANSAS
ARIZONA
CALIFORNIA
DELAWARE
FLORIDA
ILLINOIS
IOWA
KANSAS
MAINE
MARYLAND
MINNESOTA
MISSOURI
MONTANA
NEBRASKA
NEW YORK
NORTH DAKOTA
OHIO
OREGON
RHODE ISLAND
TENNESSEE
TEXAS
UTAH
VERMONT
WYOMING

Feeling Dotty 3

Connect the dots below, in order, and you will draw a flag of one of the U.S. states. Can you identify which state's it is? If not, you may decode the answer by anagramming the letters that have not been crossed out once the dots are connected.

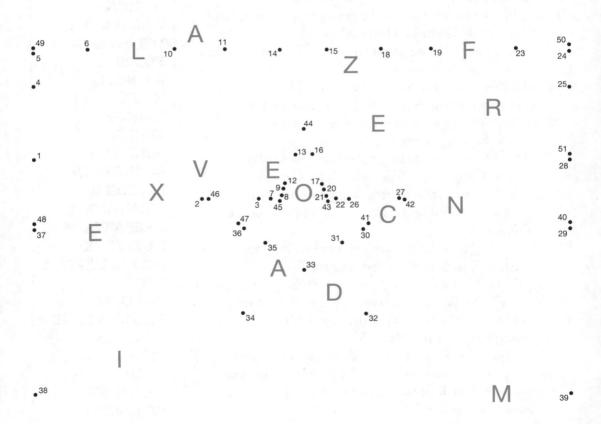

All Over the Map 10

Can you determine the reasoning used to enumerate the states in the map below? The rationale may be geographical, logological, historical, or anything else.

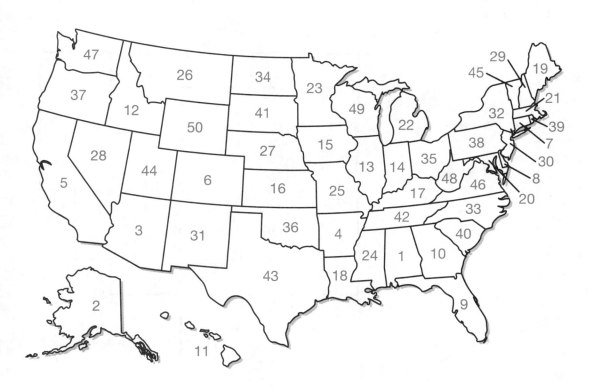

Pentomino Puzzle: Ohio

Pentominoes are geometric shapes formed by adjoining five squares edge to edge. There are twelve different pentomino shapes (shown below left), which may be rotated or flipped over or both. Can you arrange the twelve pentominoes to make the shape of Ohio? Multiple solutions are possible. (If you do not have physical pentomino pieces, see Appendix C.)

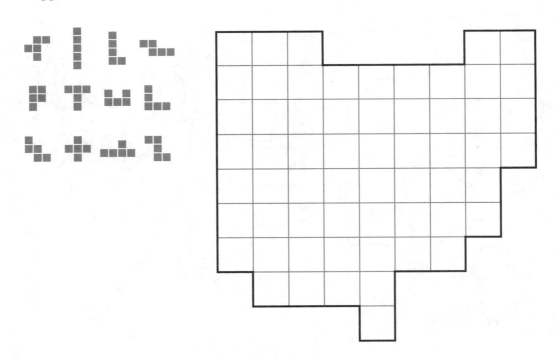

County Lines: Vermont

The names of all 14 counties of Vermont are hidden in the grid below (vertically, horizontally, diagonally, and reversed), ignoring spaces. After you find them all, the leftover letters will spell a fact about Vermont.

```
    V W I N D S O R E B R M
    O A N T H R A S E A P A
  X E S S E L P R N O X I
  W I H M E A T N A E N L
    I I A Y O I N D O E D
    A N I R N Y C D O W
  P S G D G E R E I F
  O U T T H R L L S P
  D E O O P A L L O E
    N N T C H M I N
  E H A E H I G O
  H E N L I S T M
    R I S T A T A
    L I T U E L
    K D E G R
    N N N I O
  I A A D N T
  H R R E E
  O F G N U S
```

ADDISON
BENNINGTON
CALEDONIA
CHITTENDEN
ESSEX
FRANKLIN
GRAND ISLE
LAMOILLE
ORANGE
ORLEANS
RUTLAND
WASHINGTON
WINDHAM
WINDSOR

A Commonplace Puzzle 3

Below, five state outlines have been overlaid atop one another (they are not drawn with a consistent scale). The dot represents a city, town, or village at that location within each particular state. The place's name is the same for all of the states. Can you identify the locale? Here's more help: The sixth letters of each state's name may be anagrammed into the name of the highlighted location.

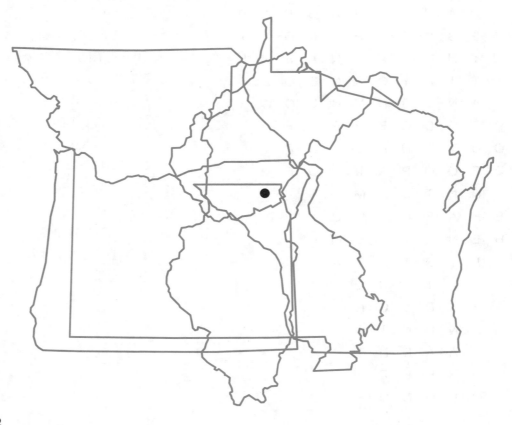

All Roads Lead to Washington, D.C. ★★★

Though America was founded as a union of separate states, each is linked to the nation's capital by a complex set of connections (which can sometimes feel like a bureaucratic maze). The red dot in the maze below indicates the location of the District of Columbia. Estimate your hometown's location on the map, and from that point there will be exactly one path that gets you to Washington, D.C. (Of course, if you live close to the capital, this may be a rather trivial path. In that case you might try to trace a route from a more distant city instead, such as San Francisco, California.) In fact, this maze being "perfect," between any two points there will always be one, and only one, way to travel from one to the other through the labyrinth.

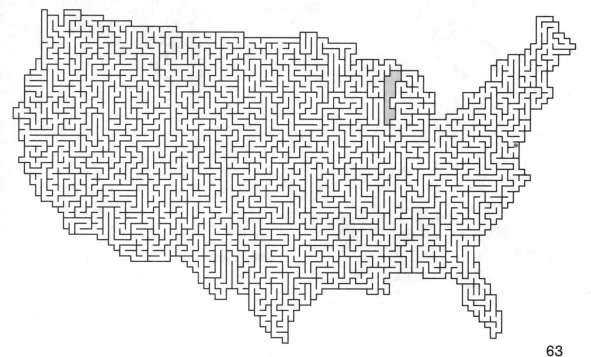

Capital Cartoons 4

The capitals of two different states are depicted below in rebus form. Can you guess the city names (and name the states of which they are the capitals)?

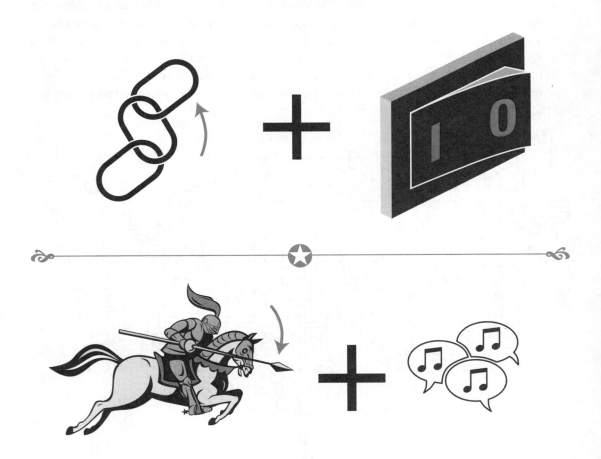

All Over the Map 11

Can you determine the reasoning used to enumerate the states in the map below? The rationale may be geographical, logological, historical, or anything else. If you're stuck, check the Hints section for a clue.

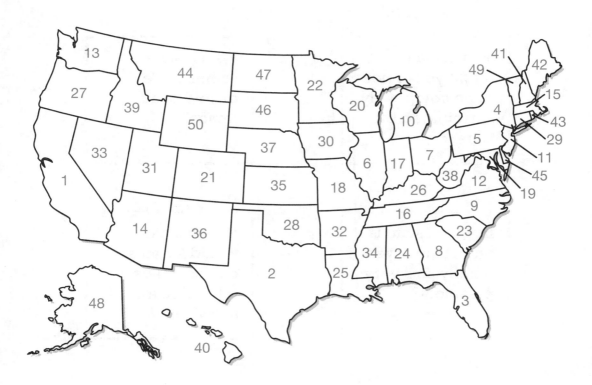

Abbreviated Answers

If I were to ask "In which state is everything generally all right?," you might answer "Oklahoma" since its postal abbreviation is OK ("okay"). With that example in mind, how might you answer the four questions below?

1. Which state might you expect to be completely surrounded by water?

2. Which state seems to be devoid of all things?

3. In which state is one of the seven deadly sins very prevalent?

4. Which state would be an apt choice to host a television award show?

All Over the Map 12

Can you determine the reasoning used to enumerate the states in the map below? The rationale may be geographical, logological, historical, or anything else. If you're stuck, check the Hints section for a clue.

Compressed States

Consider the following sequence of letters:

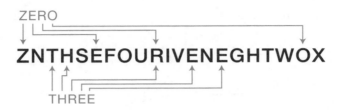

The letters are arranged so that the spelled-out versions of all ten digits, 0 through 9, can be read in order from left to right, though the letters may not necessarily be adjacent. (ZERO and THREE are highlighted as examples.)

In this case, it required a sequence of twenty-one letters to "compress" all ten words into a single string. Your challenge is to create a similar sequence of letters—but instead of digits, you must compress all 50 U.S. state names. It will, of course, require a much longer string of letters. But how many letters? Well, that's for you to experiment with and find out. If you can keep the length of the string under 100, you're doing pretty well. If you can use fewer than 90 letters, that's excellent.

I've managed to do it in 79 letters; see if you can match or beat that!

Pentomino Puzzle: New York

Pentominoes are geometric shapes formed by adjoining five squares edge to edge. There are twelve different pentomino shapes (shown below), which may be rotated or flipped over or both. Can you arrange the twelve pentominoes to make the shape of New York? Multiple solutions are possible. (If you do not have physical pentomino pieces, see Appendix C.)

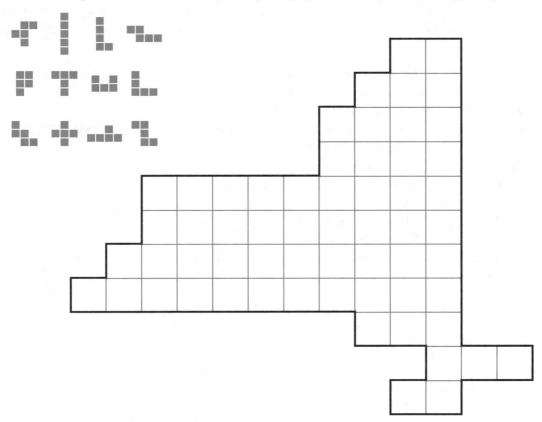

Perplex-cities: Fruits

An earlier puzzle in this book (on page 27) created imaginative city monikers by anagramming the real names of locations which contained colors. This is a similar puzzle, except this time the original names of the places contain common fruits instead of colors.

Eleven fictitious geographical sobriquets are given below. Can you unscramble the letters to reveal the actual city names?

1. **Graven Pie**, Texas (a city of 46,334 people, according to the 2010 census)
2. **Norvil Beach**, Mississippi (a city of 33,484)
3. **Long Remove**, California (a city of 25,320)
4. **Richly Revel**, North Carolina (a city of 5,760)
5. **Waters Gone**, Texas (a city of 3,443)
6. **One Spar**, Georgia (a city of 2,117)
7. **Pretty-in-Barrows**, Iowa (a city of 1,279)
8. **Percel Peak**, Ohio (a village of 1,173)
9. **Miss Pringle**, Iowa (a city of 505)
10. **Kale Lump**, Wisconsin (a town of 491)
11. **Hard Chop Acre**, Arkansas (a city of 135 people)

Nine States

Below I have labeled the rows and columns of a sample 3×3 grid with six different letters of the alphabet. In the grid's cells, if a two-letter postal abbreviation for a U.S. state can be created with the two corresponding letters for that cell's row and column, then I have written in that abbreviation. My example is not perfect, however, since there is no abbreviation that can fill several of the cells.

How can you label the second grid (again, with six different letters of the alphabet) so that all nine cells can be successfully filled with a state abbreviation?

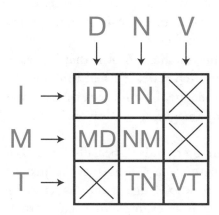

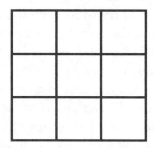

71

Rendezvous Point

This activity is not a puzzle, but rather a simple game that is perfect to initiate at a party of a dozen or so friends. This is exactly how I first heard about it, and the conversation that ensued lasted well over an hour. The next time you find yourself among many friends, see how long it keeps you entertained. Here it is:

Begin by mentioning one of the 50 states—say, Missouri. Now, imagine that someone has asked you to meet them in that state, but for whatever reason, they never specified where to meet. Maybe part of the message was lost, maybe they forgot to say; the reason is not important. What is important is that you know you are supposed to rendezvous with that someone somewhere in the state of Missouri.

Assuming that you cannot make further contact with this person before the time of the meeting, where should you go? Where, within the state of Missouri, do you think is the most likely spot someone might ask you to meet them?

Of course, this is a very contrived question, but the heart of it is that it is asking the players to try to identify the most iconic spot in each state. If I had to name the most famous, recognizable spot in Missouri to meet someone, I would pick the Gateway Arch in St. Louis (and, obviously, I'm hoping that my imaginary rendezvous partner will be thinking of that same spot).

But this can lead to a very lively discussion among friends (especially if many of them are from different parts of the United States). There are no wrong answers, just different opinions: opinions formed by personal preferences, knowledge of various states' histories and cultures, and so much more. I think Missouri is an example of a state with a pretty definitive answer; the Arch is quite iconic. But maybe not? Perhaps you will feel there is a better answer.

Other states can be more difficult for polar opposite reasons: either no one can think of an iconic spot within that state (in which case they may just default to that state's capitol building), or there are too many strong choices. (Where would you show up if you knew you had to rendezvous with someone in California? The Golden Gate Bridge? The "Hollywood" sign? The entrance to Joshua Tree National Park?) Furthermore, people native to a particular state might have wildly different answers than people who are not as familiar with that area.

Again, there are no wrong answers; this is just an exercise to stimulate discussion among friends (or strangers). After one particular state is discussed thoroughly, another is then called out and the conversation begins anew with that place in mind. ("What about Mississippi? Where do we go there?")

As I said, such discussions entertained a group of my acquaintances for a whole evening (although perhaps we were all just geography nerds). With luck, the game can amuse you and your friends in a similar fashion.

Trivial Statements 3

Here are some more trivia questions, all concerning the origins of U.S. state names.

1. Which state name is derived from the French phrase for "green mountain"?

2. Which is the only state named after its founder's father?

3. Which state name derives from the phrase "thicket clearers" in the Choctaw language?

4. How many states are named in honor of European monarchs?

5. Which state was named after a fictional place from a Spanish novel?

6. Which states' names originate from the Sioux word for "friend"?

7. The Spanish word for "snow-covered" led to the name of which state?

8. Which state, with a name derived from a native tribe, passed a state law in 1881 to make the correct pronunciation of its name official?

All Over the Map 13

Can you determine the reasoning used to enumerate the states in the map below? The rationale may be geographical, logological, historical, or anything else. If you're stuck, check the Hints section for a clue.

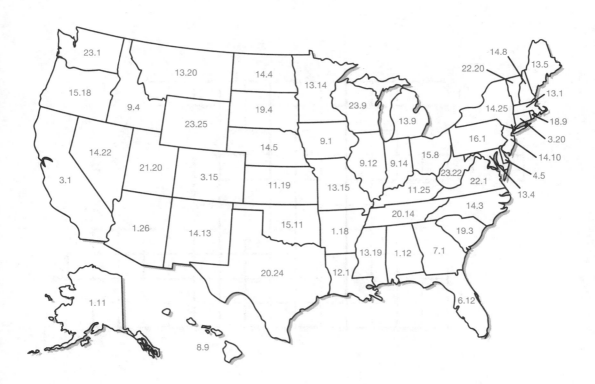

Popularity Contest: Florida

Florida is the third most populous state in the United States. Below is a blanked-out list of the 10 most populous cities of the Sunshine State, sorted by population with the largest at the top. Can you fill in the proper city names? If two or more vertically aligned cells share the same letter, they have been merged.

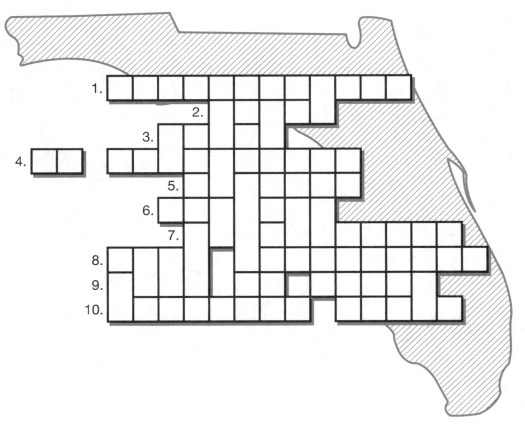

Perfectly Stated Puzzles 2

Here are more clues for words spelled solely from two-letter postal abbreviations (see page 9 for more detailed instructions, if needed). How many of them can you answer?

Two-state answers:
- Killer whale ___ ___
- Parts of some chairs ___ ___
- Acquire ___ ___
- Mark of a past wound ___ ___
- Heat before eating ___ ___
- Wind instrument? ___ ___
- Declare to be untrue ___ ___
- Reach the runway ___ ___
- Repair, as clothing ___ ___
- A generously ample amount ___ ___

Three-state answers:
- Earnings ___ ___ ___
- Like the fragrance of many perfumes ___ ___ ___
- Waifish girl ___ ___ ___
- Place to play pinball ___ ___ ___
- Speaking frankly ___ ___ ___
- Large vulture common to California ___ ___ ___
- Llama-like animal ___ ___ ___

Four-state answers:
- Most common Chinese dialect ___ ___ ___ ___
- Washington and Lincoln each have one ___ ___ ___ ___

Buried Treasure

Did I ever tell you about my rich, eccentric uncle Bob? He and his wife, Carol, passed away a few years back, but before doing so, they drove all around the country and, somewhere, buried a fortune in gold coins. Or so says the family lore. I'm not sure I believe all the tales about Uncle Bob, but just yesterday I received the following letter in the mail. It seems to be part of a journal my uncle kept while on his final road trip. Given the strange tone and weird events described, I have no doubt it was indeed written by Uncle Bob.

August 17, 2015

Over months Carol and I travel through many states and have many more gonzo adventures. For example, during the third week of June we spot a tornado, and I take this vortex as a sign that we should stop for the day (plus, a weather bulletin on the radio warns of continuing thunderstorms throughout the day).

Minutes later we pull into the parking lot of a roadside diner. With the exception of a teenage girl, the place is devoid of customers. This young miss is sipping a cola and keeping an eye on her dog (a mongrel, partly a lab—a mangy mutt, really) that's sniffing about outside.

"You'll find Ian at the drive-in!" shouts a voice from the kitchen, apparently the only waitress working at the moment. "Don't leave the washing to Nathan!" she continues (yelling at the cook?), "Ian's supposed to be doing the dishes!" Finally she sees us as we sit at a booth. (We remain, even though Carol is starting to have serious reservations about eating a meal here.)

Sauntering over, Lori (so reads her nametag) acts nonchalant and strikes the aloof pose of a supermodel (aware that she should be happy to have some paying customers?). Before she gets out a "hello," "hi," or "howdy," though, everything goes nuts.

The ugly dog (seriously, it's an uncommon tan and orange color; a downright filthy thing) wanders into the restaurant; its jaws about a huge (or giant!) dead thing, reeking of rottenness.

"Eek!" screams the girl with the soda, and off Lori dashes to the kitchen. The mutt drops the carcass (how best to describe the thing, "sinewy" or "knotted"?) in the middle of the diner and seems to be waiting for praise from someone.

As for Carol and I? We dismiss our intense hunger and decide lunch can wait. Back in the car, she takes the wheel, but seems uncertain which way to drive.

"Just go north, Carol." In a state of shock still, I noisily slam the car door and fumble to turn the radio back on...

With the journal entry came a short note: "I buried my coins in one of the lower 48 states. The treasure is hidden on the grounds of the state capitol building. Which state? Well, it's not named in this journal entry nor does it border any state mentioned therein. Dig six feet west of the flagpole. Good luck!"

That's all well and good, I suppose, but I don't see any states mentioned in the story above. Maybe you can make more sense of this than I can? In which state did Uncle Bob bury his wealth?

Pentomino Puzzle: West Virginia

Pentominoes are geometric shapes formed by adjoining five squares edge to edge. There are twelve different pentomino shapes (shown below), which may be rotated or flipped over or both. Can you arrange the twelve pentominoes to make the shape of West Virginia? Multiple solutions are possible. (If you do not have physical pentomino pieces, see Appendix C.)

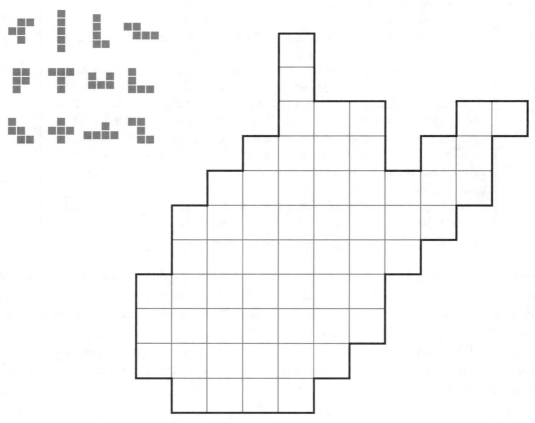

County Lines: New Mexico

The names of all 33 counties of New Mexico are hidden in the grid below (vertically, horizontally, diagonally, and reversed), ignoring spaces and diacritical marks. After you find them all, the leftover letters will spell a fact about New Mexico.

```
N E S O M A L A S O L W M Y E
X S I A C U O E L N S S R A O
T A A T N E R L F L O R L U R
A N G A F D I E A O U T Y Q R
S M O R A L O T U C R E E S O
A I S I A U A V A N N P L R C
S G E N N C R T A I U Y N C O
M U R R I U R O G L A D I H S
B E O B R O I O A L S O K A A
B L O T N A B D H A A N C V N
H L S T A C A B E D N A M E J
A O E R I U G I N A T A O S U
R T V D G E T O R R A N C E A
D D E I D N Z C O L F A X I N
I A L P U Y E V A L E N C I A
N B T N A R G
G L O
```

BERNALILLO
CATRON
CHAVES
CIBOLA
COLFAX
CURRY
DE BACA
DOÑA ANA
EDDY
GRANT
GUADALUPE
HARDING
HIDALGO
LEA
LINCOLN
LOS ALAMOS
LUNA

MCKINLEY
MORA
OTERO
QUAY
RIO ARRIBA
ROOSEVELT
SANDOVAL
SAN JUAN
SAN MIGUEL
SANTA FE
SIERRA
SOCORRO
TAOS
TORRANCE
UNION
VALENCIA

All Over the Map 14

Can you determine the reasoning used to enumerate the states in the map below? The rationale may be geographical, logological, historical, or anything else. If you're stuck, check the Hints section for a clue.

Capital Cartoons 5

The capitals of two different states are depicted below in rebus form. Can you guess the city names (and name the states of which they are the capitals)?

Pentomino Puzzle: Missouri ★★★

Pentominoes are geometric shapes formed by adjoining five squares edge to edge. There are twelve different pentomino shapes (shown at right), which may be rotated or flipped over or both. Can you arrange the twelve pentominoes to make the shape of Missouri? Multiple solutions are possible. (If you do not have physical pentomino pieces, see Appendix C.)

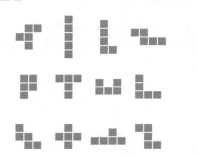

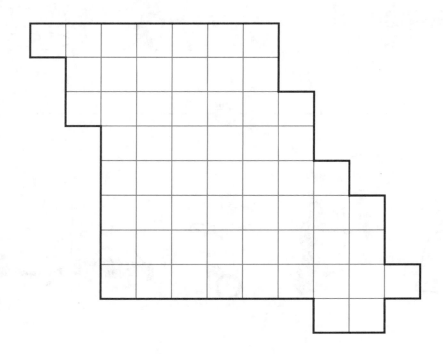

State Assembly 4

When the nine jigsaw puzzles pieces shown below are assembled, the red figure will form a silhouette of one of the 50 states (with its capital indicated by a star). Can you determine which state it is? If you have a hard time mentally moving the pieces about, you may try using some tracing paper to reconstruct the pieces into an assembled solution.

In a Mixed-Up State

The answer to each clue below is formed by mixing up (that is, anagramming) the letters of one of the 50 state names. Spaces indicate the number of letters in the answers. The answers start out as common words, but then become phrases that may be nonsensical. For example, the answer to the clue "What a G-rated movie has, unlike a horror movie" would be NO GORE (an anagram of Oregon).

- Death's counterpart in unavoidability   _ _ _ _ _ _

- Japanese-style cartoons   _ _ _ _ _

- Proposes as a candidate   _ _ _ _ _ _ _ _ _

- Deteriorated lock opener   _ _ _ _ _   _ _ _

- "My muscles are sore!"   "_ _   _ _ _ _ _ _ !"

- The smell of anthracite   _ _ _ _   _ _ _ _

- Region where you'll hear ribald remarks   _ _ _ _   _ _ _ _

- Fled in a crazed terror   _ _ _   _ _ _ _ _

- Answer to "Do you know singer Morissette's first name, monsieur?"

                                          "_ _ _ ,   _ _ _ _ _ _ "

- Had a blindfold on, say   _ _ _   _ _ _ _ _ _

- Leather seat used to ride a giant herbivore   _ _ _ _ _ _   _ _ _ _ _ _

- Couldn't keep from inviting on a date   _ _ _   _ _   _ _ _ _   _ _ _ _

- Quiet remark from someone macho   _ _ - _ _ _   _ _ _ _ _ _ _

- Relative social positions in the abyss community

                                          _ _ _ _ _   _ _ _ _ _ _

- Brian Williams, e.g., before a jury   _ _ _ _ _ _ _   _ _   _ _ _ _ _

All Over the Map 15

Can you determine the reasoning used to enumerate the states in the map below? The rationale may be geographical, logological, historical, or anything else. If you're stuck, check the Hints section for a clue.

State the Facts 3

On the first day of class, Ms. Quincy, the geography teacher, met eleven of her new students as they were dropped off by their parents.

She was concerned she might have a problem remembering all of their names, since they were being introduced to her so quickly. However, she noticed as she met them that, by a strange coincidence, the first and last initials of each child formed a two-letter postal code for a U.S. state, which helped serve as a mnemonic device.

Using the information below, can you also determine the full names of all eleven students?

1. The students' first names, in alphabetical order, were Adam, Charles, Daniel, Isabel, Megan, Nicole, Oscar, Peter, Thomas, Wanda, and Vincent.

2. The students' last names, in alphabetical order, were Andrews, Davidson, Evans, Ivanovich, North, Ortega, Richardson, Smith, Torbert, Young, and Zimmermann.

Pentomino Puzzle: Minnesota

Pentominoes are geometric shapes formed by adjoining five squares edge to edge. There are twelve different pentomino shapes (shown below), which may be rotated or flipped over or both. Can you arrange the twelve pentominoes to make the shape of Minnesota? Multiple solutions are possible. (If you do not have physical pentomino pieces, see Appendix C.)

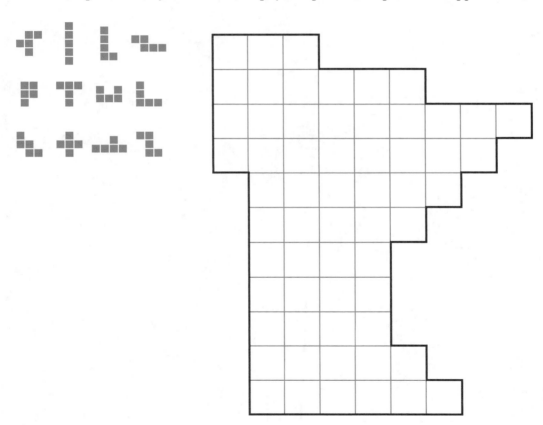

Feeling Dotty 4

Connect the dots below, in order, and you will draw a flag of one of the U.S. states. Can you identify which state's it is? If not, you may decode the answer by anagramming the letters that have not been crossed out once the dots are connected.

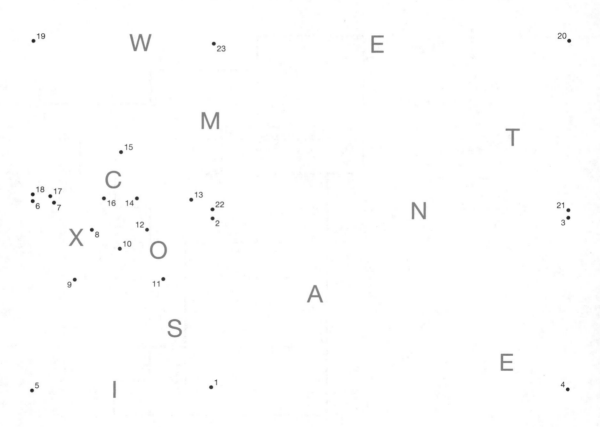

County Lines: Oregon

The names of all 36 counties of Oregon are hidden in the grid below (vertically, horizontally, diagonally, and reversed), ignoring spaces. After you find them all, the leftover letters will spell a fact about Oregon.

BAKER

BENTON

CLACKAMAS

CLATSOP

COLUMBIA

COOS

CROOK

CURRY

DESCHUTES

DOUGLAS

GILLIAM

GRANT

HARNEY

HOOD RIVER

JACKSON

JEFFERSON

JOSEPHINE

KLAMATH

LAKE

LANE

LINCOLN

LINN

MALHEUR

MARION

MORROW

MULTNOMAH

POLK

SHERMAN

TILLAMOOK

UMATILLA

UNION

WALLOWA

WASCO

WASHINGTON

WHEELER

YAMHILL

```
          T T M
          H I U E                           S N O I R A M
          T A L T               E O R O O L I N C O L N N
          C K T L O F S E T U H C S E D H O R R E
          G O N N A I S T N H E K S K T O R H U N
          D C O L U M B I A E C R E A W O L L A W
          G G M A A S O P H A E R B L W D I L D
          C A A L L N R O J Y O C A K L R L F O
      I L J H T A M A L K R E L K E D I W W U I
      T H E C H A A L C E R D N E O T V H N G Y
      T U F H A T I C N I U L S R A O E E M L F
  T R E F N N C L C L A C K A M A S R E O A L
  O R F E U O A L L O A M N U N D H P L A S Y
  T N A R G T T I T E O R R N E E D A E N D P
  W H I S S N C G H C A S N E B E H C R O O K
  O L J O S E P H I N E L O W H L N N I L I K
      E P N A B G E N O T G N I H S A W K O D E
```

Americans love their cars, and Americans love their home states. Vanity license plates on motor vehicles are often used to creatively express these sentiments. Can you identify the states of the drivers who have adorned their cars with the following plates?

GRDNST8	SUNSHYN	BHYVST8	MPYRST8
VOLNTR	JHWKST8	L1 STR	10KLAYX
GLDNST8	HWKIST8	♥OVDXE	BVR ST8
BUCKIII	CRNHSKR	PCH ST8	HUZRST8
1ST ST8	IZ4LVRS	BAJRST8	GR&CNYN

Trivial Statements 4

No theme this time, just some more trivia questions with which to test yourself or your friends.

1. Officially, four of the U.S. "states" are, in fact, designated as "commonwealths." How many of them can you name?

2. Which four U.S. states have no parts of their borders defined by water features (rivers, lakes, oceans, etc)?

3. Which state's flag is not rectangular in shape?

4. According to official government specifications, if a flag of the United States is 20 inches high, how long should it be?

5. In 2013 one of the Best Picture nominees for the Academy Awards was a film whose one-word title was the name of a state. The year prior, in 2012, there was a Best Picture nominee whose one-word title was the capital of that state. (Neither won the award.) What were the names of the films?

6. Speaking of movies, of all the movies whose title contains a U.S. state, which has grossed the most money at the U.S. domestic box office (not adjusted for inflation)?

7. What is the highest-grossing film that includes the word "state" in its title?

All Over the Map 16

Can you determine the reasoning used to enumerate the states in the map below? The rationale may be geographical, logological, historical, or anything else. If you're stuck, check the Hints section for a clue.

First and Last

Consider the following city names: Aurora (Colorado), Norman (Oklahoma), and Sparks (Nevada). Each begins and ends with a matching letter (A, N, and S, respectively). Your challenge is to try to think of more such cities, one for each letter of the alphabet (except for J, Q, U, V, X, and Z, for which no examples exist). You'll earn points for each one you think of, and to maximize your score, you should try to think of city names that are as long as possible. Write your answers below and record their lengths (don't count spaces and don't include state names). When finished, add up all of the lengths to get your grand total. A score over 50 is fair, over 100 is good, over 150 is very good, and over 200 is excellent. My best score is given in the Answers section.

	city	length		city	length
A	_____	____	L	_____	____
B	_____	____	M	_____	____
C	_____	____	N	_____	____
D	_____	____	O	_____	____
E	_____	____	P	_____	____
F	_____	____	R	_____	____
G	_____	____	S	_____	____
H	_____	____	T	_____	____
I	_____	____	W	_____	____
K	_____	____	Y	_____	____

Popularity Contest: New York

New York is the fourth most populous state in the United States (and is home to the biggest city in the nation as a whole). Below is a blanked-out list of the 10 most populous cities of the Empire State, sorted by population with the largest at the top. Can you fill in the proper city names? If two or more vertically aligned cells share the same letter, they have been merged.

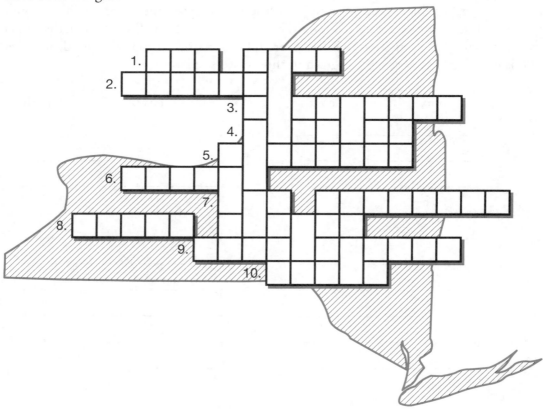

Squared Away 3

Clues are provided to help you complete the small crossword puzzles below. However, each answer is a six-letter word or phrase, and some of the cells must have two letters written in them. Any such bigrams entered will be two-letter postal abbreviations of U.S. states.

1	2	3	4
5			
6			
7			

ACROSS

1 Crocs' cousins
5 Area in which you might write notes
6 Chant
7 Acquire with effort

DOWN

1 Playing the slots, e.g.
2 Cream of ___
3 Theoretical form of energy proposed by Wilhelm Reich (and which is an anagram of a state name)
4 Person visiting a confessional

1	2	3	4
5			
6			
7			

ACROSS

1 Heavily embroiled
5 Key with two flats
6 Costumed character on the sidelines
7 Give everyone a hand again

DOWN

1 Swedish film director Bergman
2 Undoing
3 Make harder to read, in a way
4 Grand entryway

A Commonplace Puzzle 4

Below, six state outlines have been overlaid atop one another (they are not drawn with a consistent scale). The dot represents a city, town, or village at that location within each particular state. The place's name is the same for all of the states. Can you identify the locale? Here's more help: The fourth letters of each state's name may be anagrammed into the name of the highlighted location.

All Over the Map 17

Can you determine the reasoning used to enumerate the states in the map below? The rationale may be geographical, logological, historical, or anything else. If you're stuck, check the Hints section for a clue.

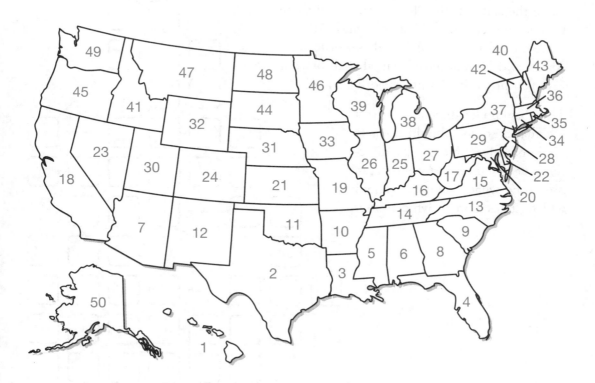

Borderline Crazy

★★★☆

In the diagram below right each square represents a U.S. state. Red lines between squares indicate that those particular states share a border (for the purpose of this puzzle you may assume the states at the "four corners" all share proper borders; i.e., Colorado and Arizona share a border, as do Utah and New Mexico). Alaska and Hawaii have been labeled for you. Can you properly identify the other states?

The diagram is only an abstract schematic, so you should not rely on knowledge of compass directions or distances between states; use only what is known about which states border which other states.

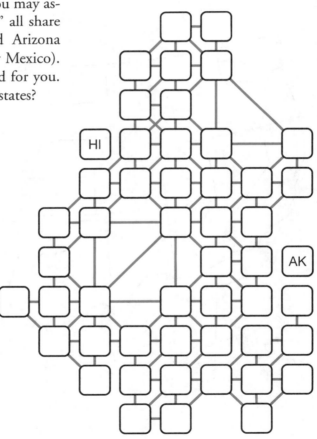

State Assembly 5

When the twelve jigsaw puzzles pieces shown below are assembled, the red figure will form a silhouette of one of the 50 states (with its capital indicated by a star). Can you determine which state it is? If you have a hard time mentally moving the pieces about, you may try using some tracing paper to reconstruct the pieces into an assembled solution.

County Lines: Wyoming

The names of all 23 counties of Wyoming are hidden in the grid below (vertically, horizontally, diagonally, and reversed), ignoring spaces. After you find them all, the leftover letters will spell a fact about Wyoming.

```
S W Y O E M C N K O O R C I N
U G G S I F A R A R B O I N L
B T N O M E R F A T N G E O F
L N E I A A B T U V R H R T E
E R S I R T O S E S S O T E A
T O K R A P N R T O E M N T P
T H Y T L A S M G M A O L A L
E G N S W E E T W A T E R T A
H I A E A M E N O S N H O J T
U B B N A D I R E H S R I C T
A N L B I S O W A S H A K I E
N C A M P B E L L I N C O L N
```

ALBANY
BIG HORN
CAMPBELL
CARBON
CONVERSE
CROOK
FREMONT
GOSHEN
HOT SPRINGS
JOHNSON
LARAMIE
LINCOLN
NATRONA
NIOBRARA
PARK
PLATTE
SHERIDAN
SUBLETTE
SWEETWATER
TETON
UINTA
WASHAKIE
WESTON

Unstated Reasoning

In this book's introduction I wrote about puzzle parties that I have organized. This puzzle is similar to the type of challenges that players at those events would encounter. Sometimes such puzzles have cryptic (or nonexistent) instructions, and the biggest challenge is simply trying to figure out what approach you must use to solve it. In this puzzle, the answer you are looking for is a single word that refers to a type of geometric object. Can you figure out what it is?

One advantage you have over a solver encountering this puzzle with no context is that you know this book's theme and thus have a general idea what the puzzle's subject might be. However, if you want further help, check the Hints section.

Feeling Dotty 5

Connect the dots below, in order, and you will draw a flag of one of the U.S. states. Can you identify which state's it is? If not, you may decode the answer by anagramming the letters that have not been crossed out once the dots are connected.

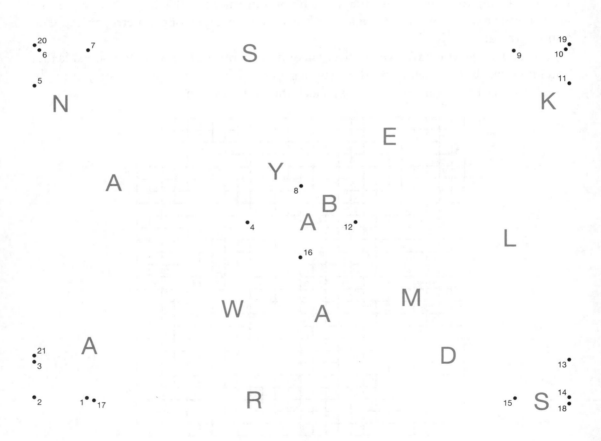

Probable States

Imagine that you have two dice with blank sides. You're allowed to pick twelve different letters of the alphabet and distribute those letters however you wish among the faces of the two cubes. Your goal, when rolling the pair of dice, is to have the greatest chance of rolling one of the 50 two-letter postal abbreviations of the states. The order of the dice does not matter; you may decide, after a roll, which die is used for the first letter and which for the second. Which twelve letters of the alphabet do you choose and upon which die do you place each? (Remember that all twelve letters must be different.)

If you're unsure how to approach this challenge, see the Hints section for a suggestion.

A Commonplace Puzzle 5

Below, seven state outlines have been overlaid atop one another (they are not drawn with a consistent scale). The dot represents a city, town, or village at that location within each particular state. The place's name is the same for all of the states. Can you identify the locale? Here's more help: The first letters of each state's name may be anagrammed into the name of the highlighted location.

Pentomino Puzzle: The Lower 48 ★★★

Pentominoes are geometric shapes formed by adjoining five squares edge to edge. There are twelve different pentomino shapes (shown at right), which may be rotated or flipped over or both. Can you arrange the twelve pentominoes to make the shape of the lower 48 states? Multiple solutions are possible. (If you do not have physical pentomino pieces, see Appendix C.)

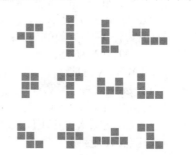

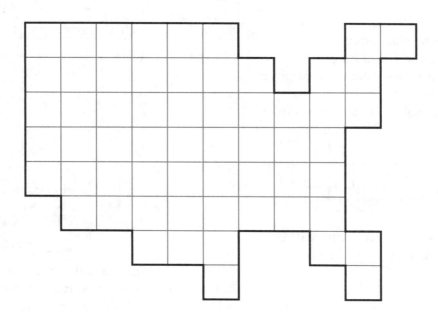

8. The unique solution is shown at right:

9. Two states: INKS, LAVA, ARID, WAND, COAL, OHMS, COIN, MAIL.
   Three states: INVADE, ALARMS, VANDAL, NECTAR, MODEMS, DECODE.
   Four states: CALAMARI, MALARIAL.

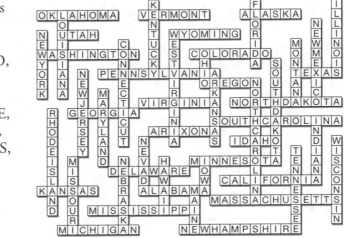

10. Each value indicates the number of states sharing a border with the given state.

11. One solution (of 235 possible):

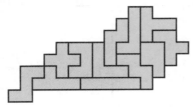

12. Jackson (jacks + sun), Mississippi; Boise (boys + E), Idaho.

13.

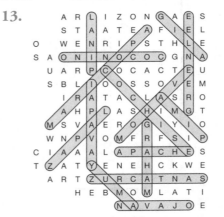

Arizona's state flower is the saguaro cactus blossom. It also has its very own official state neckwear, the bola tie.

14. Colorado:

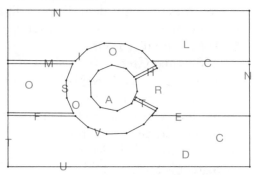

15. The states are ranked by land area, from largest to smallest.

16. Helen Columbus from Ohio,
Frank Denver from Kentucky,
Paul Jackson from Mississippi,
June Lincoln from Alaska,
Harris Montgomery from Alabama.

17. Lee (in Florida, New Hampshire, and New York).

18. Idaho:

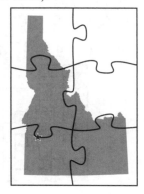

19. One solution (of 14 possible):

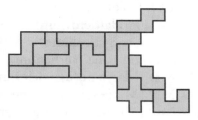

20. Numbers represent each state's number of presidential electoral votes (as of 2020).

21. Los Angeles, San Diego, San Jose, San Francisco, Fresno, Sacramento, Long Beach, Oakland, Bakersfield, Anaheim.

22.

DE	CA	F
AR	B	OR
S	IN	KS

S	PA	DE
WA	NE	S
MI	L	KS

23. 1. Only one: Alabama.
2. Only one: New York.
3. With the left hand: Texas. With the right hand: Ohio. In a single row: Alaska.
4. South Dakota (whose capital is Pierre).
5. AL (Alabama/aluminum)
AR (Arkansas/argon)
[answer continues on next page]

CA (California/calcium)
CO (Colorado/cobalt)
FL (Florida/flerovium)
GA (Georgia/gallium)
LA (Louisiana/lanthanum)
MD (Maryland/mendelevium)
MN (Minnesota/manganese)
MO (Missouri/molybdenum)
MT (Montana/meitnerium)
NE (Nebraska/neon)
ND (North Dakota/neodymium)
PA (Pennsylvania/protactinium)
SC (South Carolina/scandium)
6. NE-WY-OR-KS and CO-HI-OK

24. Mo-N-Ta-Na
Ne-W-H-Am-P-S-H-I-Re
O-H-I-O
S-O-U-Th-C-Ar-O-Li-Na
U-Ta-H
Wisconsin has nine variations:
    W-I-Sc-O-N-Si-N
    W-I-Sc-O-N-S-In
    W-I-Sc-O-N-S-I-N
    W-I-S-Co-N-Si-N
    W-I-S-Co-N-S-In
    W-I-S-Co-N-S-I-N
    W-I-S-C-O-N-Si-N
    W-I-S-C-O-N-S-In
    W-I-S-C-O-N-S-I-N

26. Numbers equal the number of counties (or equivalent districts, like Louisiana's parishes) in each state.

27. 1. Brownsville, Texas
2. Bowling Green, Kentucky
3. White Plains, New York
4. Blue Island, Illinois
5. Orangeburg, South Carolina
6. Blackstone, Massachusetts
7. Redwood Falls, Minnesota
8. Yellow Springs, Ohio
9. Graysville, Alabama
10. Pink Hill, North Carolina
11. Purple Sage, Wyoming

28.

$$
\begin{array}{r}
65682 \\
+\,981849 \\
\hline
1047531
\end{array}
$$

0 1 2 3 4 5 6 7 8 9
M A Y C E I F R T S

29. One solution (of 357 possible):

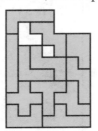

30. Juneau (June: no), Alaska; Columbus (column + bus), Ohio.
31. States are labeled with the number of syllables in their names.
32. Alton (in Maine, Illinois, Utah, Iowa, and Indiana).
33. Kentucky:

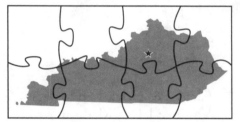

34. "Our liberties we prize, and our rights we will maintain" is the state motto of Iowa.
35.

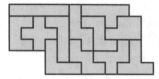

New Jersey, a.k.a. the Garden State, has more urban area by percentage than all other states.
36. The states are ordered according to their admissions into the union (earliest to latest).
37. One solution (of 3,897 possible):

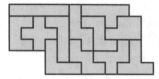

38.

DE	CA	DE
MON	D	E
N	OR	MS

LA	B	OR
P	RI	DE
IN	NE	R

39. G is the correct flag.
40. Houston, San Antonio, Dallas, Austin, Fort Worth, El Paso, Arlington, Corpus Christi, Plano, Laredo
41. Each state is labeled with the number of presidents born there. South Carolina has an asterisk because Andrew Jackson (the seventh president) was born in a yet-to-be surveyed area between North and South Carolina, but later claimed South Carolina as his birthplace.

42. At right is one of many possible 4-colorings. (In this coloring, the diagonally adjacent states at the Four Corners were treated as adjacent for coloring purposes.)

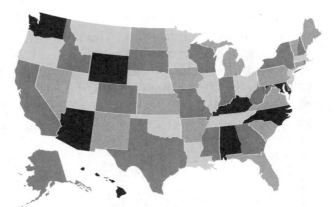

44. Concord (conch + chord), New Hampshire; Salem (sail + limb), Oregon.

45. Tennessee:

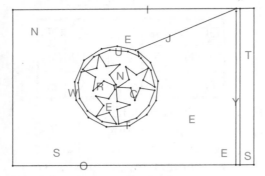

46. The unique solution:

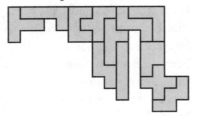

47. Charles & Helen wed in West Virginia; Jeff & Madison wed in Wisconsin; Marc & Diana wed in North Dakota; Pierre & Cheyenne wed in South Dakota; and Trent & Lulu wed in Hawaii.

48. Numbers are the values of colored properties with state names in the board game Monopoly.

49. 1. Carson City, Nevada; Jefferson City, Missouri; Oklahoma City, Oklahoma; and Salt Lake City, Utah.

2. As of the 2010 U.S. Census, the answer was Flint, Michigan. However, that city's population has been declining, and according to 2017 estimates

the answer is now Kent, Washington (or, depending on how you pronounce it, Orange, California).

3. Fresno, California. (While the major federally funded roads in Alaska and Hawaii do not connect to other states, they are officially part of the Interstate Highway System.)

4. Austin, Texas.

5. Albuquerque, New Mexico.

6. It contains more distinct letters of the alphabet (15) than any other city in the United States.

7. Oklahoma; Wisconsin.

8. Xenia (which, as of the 2010 U.S. Census, is a city of 25,719 people in Ohio, and a village of 391 people in Illinois).

50. Here is my list of twelve states, ordered alphabetically by length (blanks are indicated in red): IOWA, UTAH, IDAHO, TEXAS, NEVADA, ARIZONA, FLORIDA, GEORGIA, VERMONT, ILLINOIS, KENTUCKY, NEW JERSEY

51. Numbers indicate the length of the state names, ignoring spaces.

52. Going roughly clockwise, from the upper left: "Meet Me in Montana," "I Got a Gal I Love (In North and South Dakota)," "Indiana Wants Me," "The Devil Came Up to Michigan," "Boy From New York City," "(The Lights Went Out in) Massachusetts," "Pennsylvania 6-5000," "Meet Virginia," "Kentucky Gambler," "Tennessee," "Georgia on My Mind," "Sweet Home Alabama," "Louisiana Woman, Mississippi Man," "The Yellow Rose of Texas," "There Is No Arizona," "Hotel California," "Hawaii Five-O."

54. Missouri:

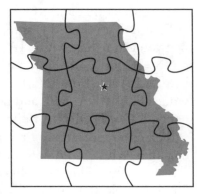

55. Q = 22. The other values are:
A = 2, B = 10, C = 6, D = 19, E = 14,
F = 18, G = 11, H = 1, I = 12,
J = 24, K = 23, L = 20, M = 9,
N = 16, O = 26, P = 25, R = 15,
S = 4, T = 21, U = 3, V = 17, W = 7,
X = 5, Y = 8, Z = 13. To get started,
note that Iowa and Hawaii share
three letters, so IOWA − HAWAII
(47 − 36) = O − HAI = 11.
OHIO = 65, so OHIO + (O − HAI) =
65 + 11 = 76 = OOO − A, and since
the maximum letter value is 26,
O must be 26, and A is 2. Next,
comparing the values of Arkansas/
Kansas and Ohio/Idaho will
determine the values of R and
D. Next, reduce NEVADA to
NEV, subtract that and RO from
VERMONT to find MT, and
then you can reduce MONTANA
to NN = 32, or N = 16. You can
then get I's value from INDIANA.
Reduce FLORIDA to FL and use
that with CALIFORNIA to find
C, then use these states to find the
remaining values: Colorado (L, and
thus also F from Florida), Ohio (H),
Illinois (S), North Carolina (T, and
thus also M from Vermont), Utah
(U), Maine (E, and thus also V from
Nevada), Texas (X), Arizona (Z),
Iowa (W), Kansas (K), Maryland
(Y), New Jersey (J), Alabama (B),
Oregon (G), Mississippi (P). By
elimination, Q can only be 22.

56. 1. AL + Maine = A.A. Milne
   2. DR + Delaware = Edward Lear
   3. FL + Nebraska = Bran Flakes
   4. GM + Iowa = mogwai
   5. GO + Maryland = Gary Oldman
   6. HI + Kansas = Kinshasa
   7. HY + New York = Kenworthy
   8. IM + Oregon = Geronimo
   9. IR + Texas = Asterix
   10. IY + Montana (plus an accent
       mark) = "My Ántonia"
   11. JN + Missouri = Junior Miss
   12. JY + Alabama = "Jambalaya"
   13. NS + Florida = dorsal fin
   14. NT + Utah = U Thant
   15. PW + Ohio = Whoopi
   16. ST + Arkansas = Sansa Stark
   17. ACR + Illinois = Sinclair Oil
   18. AES + Vermont = Moe's Tavern
   19. AGY + Wyoming = "Going
       My Way"
   20. ALM + Arizona = Mario Lanza
   21. AVY + Rhode Island =
       Harley-Davidson

22. ETV + California = African violet
23. HSU + Alaska = Lukas Haas
24. LSW + Minnesota = Winston-Salem
25. VVY + Tennessee = seventy-seven
26. EENT + North Dakota = "The Road Not Taken"

58. Arizona:

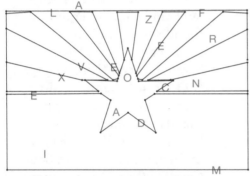

59. The states are ordered alphabetically.

60. One solution (of 1,033 possible):

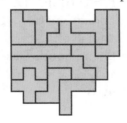

61.

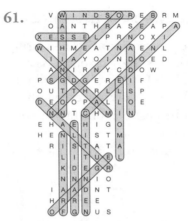

Vermont has approximately one dairy cow per four people, the highest ratio in the U.S.

62. Union (in Missouri, Wisconsin, West Virginia, Illinois, and Oregon).

64. Lincoln (link + on), Nebraska; Lansing (lance + sing), Michigan.

65. The states are ranked by population (highest to lowest, based on 2017 U.S. Census estimates).

66. 1. Illinois (IL = isle)
    2. Montana (MT = empty)
    3. Nevada (NV = envy)
    4. Maine (ME = Emmy)

67. Each state displays the number of different letters in its name (e.g., Tennessee uses E, N, S, and T).

68. My best answer consists of a string of 79 letters, shown above. As an example, ALABAMA is highlighted in red. Strings of shorter length might be possible, but I have not yet found one.

69. One solution (of 56 possible):

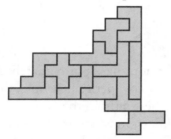

70.
1. Grapevine, Texas
2. Olive Branch, Mississippi
3. Lemon Grove, California
4. Cherryville, North Carolina
5. West Orange, Texas
6. Pearson, Georgia
7. Strawberry Point, Iowa
8. Apple Creek, Ohio
9. Lime Springs, Iowa
10. Plum Lake, Wisconsin
11. Peach Orchard, Arkansas

71.

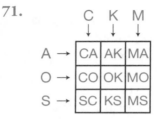

74.
1. Vermont.
2. Pennsylvania (named after Sir William Penn, father of the founder William Penn).
3. Alabama.
4. Seven: Georgia (King George II of Great Britain), Louisiana (King Louis XIV of France), Maryland (Queen Henrietta Maria, wife of King Charles of England), North and South Carolina (King Charles himself), and the two Virginias (Queen Elizabeth, the "Virgin Queen").
5. California (from "Las Sergas de Esplandián" by Garci Rodríguez de Montalvo).
6. North and South Dakota.
7. Nevada.
8. Arkansas.

75. The numbers are an alphanumerically enciphered representation of each state's two-letter postal abbreviation, with a dot separating the two numbers. For instance, Nevada (NV) is labeled 14.22 because N is the 14th letter of the alphabet and V is 22nd.

76. Jacksonville, Miami, Tampa, St. Petersburg, Orlando, Hialeah, Tallahassee, Fort Lauderdale, Port St. Lucie, Pembroke Pines.

77. Two states: ORCA, ARMS, GAIN, SCAR, COOK, VANE, DENY, LAND, MEND, MANY.
Three states: INCOME, FLORAL, GAMINE, ARCADE, CANDID, CONDOR, ALPACA.
Four states: MANDARIN, MEMORIAL.

78. The following 20 state names may be found hidden in this order within the journal's text: Vermont (oVER MONThs), Oregon (mORE GONzo), Texas (vorTEX AS), Iowa (radIO WArns), Mississippi (MISS IS SIPPIng), Alabama (A LAB A MAngy), Indiana (fIND IAN At), Washington (WASHING TO Nathan), Maine (reMAIN Even), Delaware (supermoDEL AWARE), Ohio (hellO HI Or), Montana (uncomMON TAN And), Colorado (COLOR A DOwnright), Utah (aboUT A Huge), Georgia (huGE OR GIAnt), Tennessee (rotTENNESS EEk), New York (siNEWY OR Knotted), Missouri (disMISS OUR Intense), North Carolina (NORTH CAROL IN A), and Illinois (stILL I NOISily). The only one of the lower 48 states that is neither mentioned nor borders a named state is Rhode Island, so the treasure is buried at that state's capitol building.

80. One solution (of 24 possible):

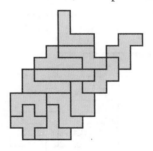

81.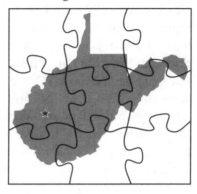

New Mexico's state flag features a sun symbol that originated in Zia Pueblo.

82. Numbers indicate the number of NFL teams that play in each state.

83. Carson City (car + sun + sit + tea), Nevada; Sacramento (sack + rah + men + tow), California.

84. One solution (of 1,007 possible):

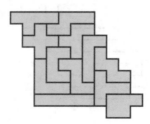

85. West Virginia:

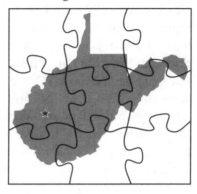

86. TAXES (Texas), ANIME (Maine), NOMINATES (Minnesota), WORN KEY (New York), "I'M ACHING!" (Michigan), COAL ODOR (Colorado), LEWD AREA (Delaware), RAN MADLY (Maryland) "OUI, ALANIS" (Louisiana), SAW NOTHING (Washington), RHINO SADDLE (Rhode Island), HAD TO ASK OUT (South Dakota), HE-MAN WHISPER (New Hampshire), CHASM STATUSES (Massachusetts), ANCHOR ON TRIAL (North Carolina)

87. Numbers represent the number of Miss America titleholders from each state, as of May 2019. (Note that the count includes both Miss Americas from 1984, New York's Vanessa Williams, who resigned, and New Jersey's Suzette Charles.)

88. Adam Zimmerman, Charles Ortega, Daniel Evans, Isabel Davidson, Megan Smith, Nicole Young, Oscar Richardson, Peter Andrews, Thomas North, Wanda Ivanovich, and Vincent Torbert.

89. One solution (of 237 possible):

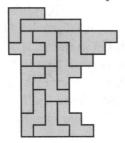

90. Texas:

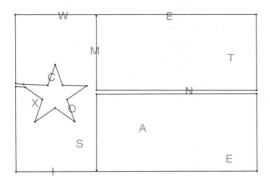

91.

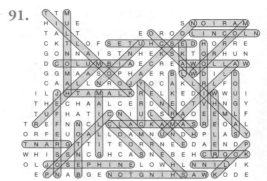

The state rock of Oregon is the thunderegg, a spherical rock filled with chalcedony that is often colorful and patterned, and which can be hollow like a geode.

92. Row by row, from top to bottom:
New Jersey ("GARDEN STATE")
Florida ("SUNSHINE" state)
Utah ("BEEHIVE STATE")
New York ("EMPIRE STATE")
Tennessee ("VOLUNTEER" state)
Kansas ("JAYHAWK STATE")
Texas ("LONE STAR" state)
Minnesota (land of "10,000 LAKES")
California ("GOLDEN STATE")
Iowa ("HAWKEYE STATE")
Alabama ("HEART OF DIXIE")
Oregon ("BEAVER STATE")
[answer continues on next page]

Ohio ("BUCKEYES")
Nebraska ("CORNHUSKER" state)
Georgia ("PEACH STATE")
Indiana ("HOOSIER STATE")
Delaware ("FIRST STATE")
Virginia ("... IS FOR LOVERS")
Wisconsin ("BADGER STATE")
Arizona ("GRAND CANYON" state)

93. 1. Kentucky, Massachusetts, Pennsylvania, and Virginia.
2. Colorado, Montana, Wyoming, and Utah.
3. Ohio.
4. 38 inches (the official specifications require the width-to-height ratio to be 1.9:1).
5. "Lincoln" (2012) and "Nebraska" (2013).
6. "Indiana Jones and the Kingdom of the Crystal Skull" (2008).
7. "Enemy of the State" (1998).

94. States are labeled with the numeric designations of the Federal Reserve Banks located within them. (Missouri has two, one in St. Louis and one in Kansas City.)

95. My best score:
Apalachicola (FL) = 12
Bald Knob (AR) = 8
Cadillac (MI) = 8
Dauphin Island (AL) = 13
Edgecliff Village (TX) = 16
Frostproof (FL) = 10
Gaithersburg (MD) = 12
Huntington Beach (CA) = 15
Isanti (MN) = 6
Kinderhook (NY) = 10
Laguna Niguel (CA) = 12
McLendon-Chisholm (TX) = 16
North Charleston (SC) = 15
Owensboro (KY) = 9
Pennington Gap (VA) = 13
Richland Center (WI) = 14
South Chicago Heights (IL) = 19
Travelers Rest (SC) = 13
West Haverstraw (NY) = 14
Yucca Valley (CA) = 11
Total: 246

96. New York, Buffalo, Rochester, Yonkers, Syracuse, Albany, New Rochelle, Mount Vernon, Schenectady, Utica.

97.

GA	T	OR	S
M	AR	G	IN
IN	T	O	NE
G	AR	NE	R

IN	DE	E	P
G	MI	N	OR
MA	S	CO	T
R	E	DE	AL

98. Canton (in Wisconsin, Texas, Connecticut, South Dakota, Ohio, and Minnesota).

99. States are ranked by the latitudes of their capital cities, from south to north.

100.

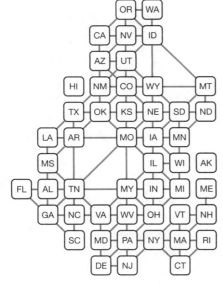

101. Massachusetts:

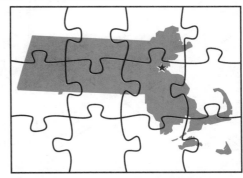

102.

```
S W Y O E M C N K O O R C I N
U G G S I F A R A R B O I N L
B T N O M E R F A T N G E O F
E N E I A A B T U V R H R T E
T R S I R T O S E S S O T E A
T H K R A P N R T O E M N T P
E G Y T L A S M G M A O L A L
H I A E A M E N O S N H O J A
U B B N A D I R E X H S R I C
A N L B I S O W A S H A K I E
N C A M P B E L L I N C O L N
```

Wyoming's flag features its state mammal, the American bison.

103. Starting from the upper left, label the rows and columns from A to Z; the stars' coordinates indicate postal codes for states (e.g., Arkansas is represented by the star at row A, column K). However, there are only 48 stars. The missing two are CO and NE, so the answer is CONE.

104. Alabama:

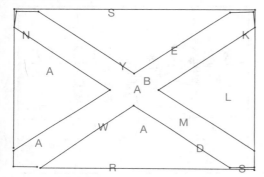

105. The highest probability I have been able to achieve is a 23 out of 36 chance (~63.9%). This can be done a few different ways; one is shown below, with dice labeled AINOST and CDHKMR, in which 23 of 36 possible rolls will result in a state abbreviation.

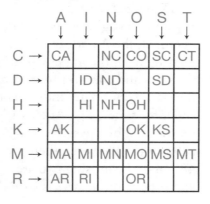

	A	I	N	O	S	T
C →	CA		NC	CO	SC	CT
D →		ID	ND		SD	
H →		HI	NH	OH		
K →	AK			OK	KS	
M →	MA	MI	MN	MO	MS	MT
R →	AR	RI		OR		

106. Clinton (in Connecticut, Louisiana, Iowa, New York, Tennessee, Oklahoma, and New Jersey). "Clinton," incidentally, is the second most common name for a municipality in the United States. Twenty-three different states have locales bearing that name within them. The most common place name is Franklin (in 26 different states).

107. One solution (of 91 possible):

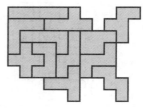

ABOUT THE AUTHOR

Eric Harshbarger has had many vocations throughout his life, including computer programmer, independent Lego brick sculptor, mathematics instructor, and, of course, puzzle designer. He lives in the 8th most populous city in the 24th most populous state. He has had a website at www.ericharshbarger.org since the mid-'90s.

HINTS

10. The rationale is geographical in nature, and can be deduced solely from studying the map.

15. Since the numbers 1 through 50 are all used exactly once, this must be a ranking of some sort.

16. Ten states border the Mississippi River: Arkansas, Illinois, Iowa, Kentucky, Louisiana, Minnesota, Mississippi, Missouri, Tennessee, and Wisconsin. Eight states border a Great Lake: Illinois, Indiana, Michigan, Minnesota, New York, Ohio, Pennsylvania, and Wisconsin. Auburn University is in Alabama, which is bordered by Florida, Georgia, Mississippi, and Tennessee.

20. Topic: Government and politics.

21. Cities #2, #3, and #4 all begin with SAN. One city is the home of Disneyland.

26. Topic: Geography.

27. Enumerations, in order, are: 11, 7 5, 5 6, 4 6, 10, 10, 7 5, 6 7, 10, 4 4, 6 4. As a general solving technique, look for colors that can be spelled using the letters in the fictional towns, then see what you can spell with what's left over, remembering that the color may be part of a longer word.

28. For S to become AM, something must be carried over from the next column. F + T is at most 17, so only a 1 can be carried over, which means S = 9, A = 1, and M = 0. Y can easily be determined next.

31. This one has a linguistic theme. Thinking out loud might help.

36. Topic: U.S. history.

40. The fifth city starts with F. One city is an anagram of ORDEAL.

41. Topic: History and politics.

48. Topic: Games.

51. This should be an easy one if you think about it for a spell.

52. The initial characters of the song titles (with state names indicated by asterisks) are, in no particular order: "*6-5," "TDCUT*," "TIN*," "H*," "*OMM," "IGAGIL(I*A**)," "BF**C," "SH*," "(TLWOI)*," "*F-O," "TYRO*," "MMI*," "*," "M*," "*WM," "*G," "*W,*M."

55. Comparing the values of IOWA, HAWAII, and OHIO is one way to get started, and will allow you to determine the values of two letters.

65. Topic: Demographics.

67. Topic: Wordplay.

70. Enumerations, in order, are: 9, 5 6, 5 5, 11, 4 6, 7, 10 5, 5 5, 4 7, 4 4, 5 7.

75. The numbering is based on a cipher, not mathematics.

76. Both two-letter segments stand for ST. Both words of city #10 start with the same letter.

78. Certain state names are "buried" in the text of the letter. For example, can you find VERMONT hidden in the first sentence?

82. Topic: Sports.

87. It might be easy to "miss" the rationale behind this one.

94. Topic: Money.

96. City #5 starts with S, the second word of city #7 starts with R, and city #8 starts with M. The letters shared within the seven merged areas are C, E (twice), N (twice), O, and Y.

99. Topic: GPS coordinates.

100. Maine is the only state that borders exactly one other state, so look for a square with one red line extending from it. Also, the Four Corners states are indicated by the only place in the schematic where two red lines cross each other.

103. How many rows and columns are there in the grid, and why might that number be signifcant? And how many stars are there?

105. Make a 6×6 grid and label each row and column with a different letter, similar to the "Nine States" puzzle on page 71, trying to maximize the number of pairings that make state abbreviations.

IMAGE CREDITS

Appendix A: Map of the United States

States (with their capital cities in parentheses) are labeled with their standard two-letter postal code abbreviations, used in many of the puzzles in this book.

AL Alabama (Montgomery)
AK Alaska (Juneau)
AZ Arizona (Phoenix)
AR Arkansas (Little Rock)
CA California (Sacramento)
CO Colorado (Denver)
CT Connecticut (Hartford)
DE Delaware (Dover)
FL Florida (Tallahassee)
GA Georgia (Atlanta)
HI Hawaii (Honolulu)
ID Idaho (Boise)
IL Illinois (Springfield)
IN Indiana (Indianapolis)
IA Iowa (Des Moines)
KS Kansas (Topeka)
KY Kentucky (Frankfort)
LA Louisiana (Baton Rouge)
ME Maine (Augusta)
MD Maryland (Annapolis)
MA Massachusetts (Boston)
MI Michigan (Lansing)
MN Minnesota (St. Paul)
MS Mississippi (Jackson)
MO Missouri (Jefferson City)
MT Montana (Helena)

NE Nebraska (Lincoln)
NV Nevada (Carson City)
NH New Hampshire (Concord)
NJ New Jersey (Trenton)
NM New Mexico (Santa Fe)
NY New York (Albany)
NC North Carolina (Raleigh)
ND North Dakota (Bismarck)
OH Ohio (Columbus)
OK Oklahoma (Oklahoma City)
OR Oregon (Salem)

PA Pennsylvania (Harrisburg)
RI Rhode Island (Providence)
SC South Carolina (Columbia)
SD South Dakota (Pierre)
TN Tennessee (Nashville)
TX Texas (Austin)
UT Utah (Salt Lake City)
VT Vermont (Montpelier)
VA Virginia (Richmond)
WA Washington (Olympia)
WV West Virginia (Charleston)
WI Wisconsin (Madison)
WY Wyoming (Cheyenne)

Appendix B: Chemical Elements

This list of chemical elements, ordered alphabetically by element, may be helpful for solving "Chemically Altered States" (p. 24–25).

Ac	Actinium	Er	Erbium	Hg	Mercury	Rf	Rutherfordium
Al	Aluminum	Eu	Europium	Mo	Molybdenum	Sm	Samarium
Am	Americium	Fm	Fermium	Mc	Moscovium	Sc	Scandium
Sb	Antimony	Fl	Flerovium	Nd	Neodymium	Sg	Seaborgium
Ar	Argon	F	Fluorine	Ne	Neon	Se	Selenium
As	Arsenic	Fr	Francium	Np	Neptunium	Si	Silicon
At	Astatine	Gd	Gadolinium	Ni	Nickel	Ag	Silver
Ba	Barium	Ga	Gallium	Nh	Nihonium	Na	Sodium
Bk	Berkelium	Ge	Germanium	Nb	Niobium	Sr	Strontium
Be	Beryllium	Au	Gold	N	Nitrogen	S	Sulfur
Bi	Bismuth	Hf	Hafnium	No	Nobelium	Ta	Tantalum
Bh	Bohrium	Hs	Hassium	Og	Oganesson	Tc	Technetium
B	Boron	He	Helium	Os	Osmium	Te	Tellurium
Br	Bromine	Ho	Holmium	O	Oxygen	Ts	Tennessine
Cd	Cadmium	H	Hydrogen	Pd	Palladium	Tb	Terbium
Ca	Calcium	In	Indium	P	Phosphorus	Tl	Thallium
Cf	Californium	I	Iodine	Pt	Platinum	Th	Thorium
C	Carbon	Ir	Iridium	Pu	Plutonium	Tm	Thulium
Ce	Cerium	Fe	Iron	Po	Polonium	Sn	Tin
Cs	Cesium	Kr	Krypton	K	Potassium	Ti	Titanium
Cl	Chlorine	La	Lanthanum	Pr	Praseodymium	W	Tungsten
Cr	Chromium	Lr	Lawrencium	Pm	Promethium	U	Uranium
Co	Cobalt	Pb	Lead	Pa	Protactinium	V	Vanadium
Cn	Copernicium	Li	Lithium	Ra	Radium	Xe	Xenon
Cu	Copper	Lv	Livermorium	Rn	Radon	Yb	Ytterbium
Cm	Curium	Lu	Lutetium	Re	Rhenium	Y	Yttrium
Ds	Darmstadtium	Mg	Magnesium	Rh	Rhodium	Zn	Zinc
Db	Dubnium	Mn	Manganese	Rg	Roentgenium	Zr	Zirconium
Dy	Dysprosium	Mt	Meitnerium	Rb	Rubidium		
Es	Einsteinium	Md	Mendelevium	Ru	Ruthenium		

Appendix C: Pentominoes

If you don't have your own set of pentominoes, photocopy this page (preferably onto cardstock) and carefully cut along the thick blue lines to create a set of your own. The pieces are the correct size to fit exactly into the puzzle diagrams.

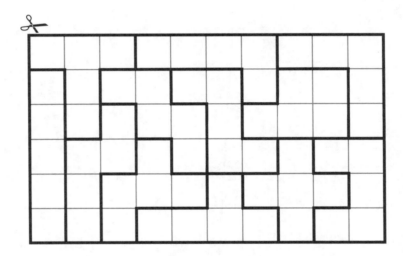